REDBONE

REDBONE

money,

malice,

and murder

in atlanta

RON STODGHILL

Amistad

An Imprint of HarperCollins*Publishers*

HarperCollins books may be purchased for educational, business, or sales promotional use. For information please write: Special Markets Department, HarperCollins Publishers, 10 East 53rd Street, New York, NY 10022.

FIRST EDITION

Designed by Laura Kaeppel

Library of Congress Cataloging-in-Publication Data

Stodghill, Ron.
    Redbone : money, malice, and murder in Atlanta / Ron Stodghill.—1st ed.
      p. cm.
    ISBN: 978-0-06-089715-4
    ISBN-10: 0-06-089715-5
    1. Herndon, Lance, d. 1996. 2. Murder—Georgia—Atlanta—Case studies. 3. African American men—Crimes against—Georgia—Atlanta. 4. Millionaires—Crimes against—Georgia—Atlanta. 5. Murder—Investigation—Georgia—Atlanta. 6. Elite (Social sciences)—Georgia—Atlanta. 7. African Americans—Georgia—Atlanta—Social life and customs. 8. Atlanta (Ga.)—Social life and customs. I. Title.

HV6534.A7S86 2007
364.152'3092—dc22   2006047716

07 08 09 10 11 BVG/RRD 10 9 8 7 6 5 4 3 2 1

For my mother,

Krisseda Ashworth Pryor

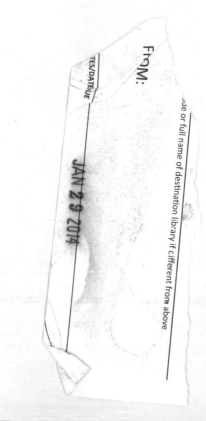

author's note

This is a work of nonfiction. Each person and event portrayed in this book is real. In a few instances, a pseudonym is used to protect the privacy of a source. Yet the material within *Redbone* is based fully upon police records, court transcripts, and interviews conducted during fact-gathering trips to Atlanta and Montego Bay, and other cities where sources knowledgeable about the case were located. There were also numerous telephone interviews with sources. But human memory and even official documents are both imperfect, often contradictory sources. While conceding to such a handicap, my goal has been to capture the truth—in facts and spirit—of events as they occurred.

Mortui vivis praecipiant

Let the dead teach the living

—Karl Rokitansky,
pioneer of
modern pathology,
circa 1860

contents

PART III

EVIDENCE OF A FEMME FATALE

prologue

It is a cold rainy afternoon in February 2003, and I am riding alongside Charles Mittelstadt in his black sport utility vehicle across the potholed streets of east Atlanta, past rows of boarded-up factories that stretch out into the hard gray distance. A lean, square-jawed man in his late thirties, Mittelstadt is a private investigator who has traded me access to his client in exchange for my own findings in the Lance Herndon case.

"So, here we are," Mittelstadt says, pulling into a crowded parking lot. "You know the rules. Anything that's gonna jeopardize her case is off-limits."

I gaze out at a colossal slab of concrete. The Fulton County Jail looks less like a building than a gigantic street curb with a door.

"Got it?"

"Yeah, I got it."

We dash through the rain into a poorly lit netherworld of justice pending, a kind of ant farm in slow motion, of waiting loved ones and lawyers, of pistol-toting officers grazing here and there, of paper-shufflers moving back and forth inside their Plexiglas, of folks cursing the long lines, emptying their pockets into metal lockers, weeping softly in their seats, and all this activity funneling down into a palpable sense of despair that leads to one place: through a heavy metal door that opens automatically and then shuts behind us with a thud of such unsettling permanence that I look back and realize that I am now sealed away with hundreds of criminals and an underpaid female guard escort who guides me through the dim concrete corridors into a small, nondescript room furnished with a jumble of metal chairs and a defunct, prehistoric-looking computer.

And this must be her standing in the doorway, her lips curled slightly in what seems to be a smirk or a bashful smile. She holds out a limp hand for me to shake, its temperature as cold as one of these cinder-block walls. She is wearing typical inmate garb—the navy blue cotton jumpsuit, with a white T-shirt beneath. Her clothing hangs off her loosely, so that her limbs protrude like metal hangers against cotton sheets.

I try to imagine what Lance Herndon saw in this woman standing here in front of me, what she looked like before the jail time. I try to imagine her laughing and talking to Lance. Cooking for him, seducing him, traveling with him, everything.

But mostly I try to imagine her murdering him.

PART I

the millionaire bachelor

chapter one

BEAUTIFUL PEOPLE

On a balmy April evening in 1996, surrounded by the thumping beat of R & B music, Lance Herndon tapped his tasseled loafer on the marble floor and watched his guests pour in. The sight must have pleased him. He had invited some four hundred friends and business associates, and by a quarter after nine more than half had already arrived. He couldn't have dreamed up a more ideal night for a party. The nightclub, a circular glass-enclosed room at the top of Atlanta's downtown Hilton Hotel, offered a panoramic view of the city. Outside, the full moon hung so low and luminous that majestic Stone Mountain, thirty miles east, glowed as though right across Peachtree Street.

The occasion tonight was the celebration of Lance's forty-first birthday. The man looked good. Except for the gray flecks in his curly dark hair, he could have easily passed for thirty. It didn't matter that he was not a particularly handsome fellow, that he had a ruddy complexion and a slightly crooked smile. He was the founder and CEO of Access Inc., the largest black computer consulting firm in the Southeast, and he exuded prosperity. On this Friday evening, Herndon was dressed casually chic. His trademark white silk pocket square blossomed like a tulip from his navy blue, single-breasted designer suit, giving him the debonair, about-town flair he was known for. His cream French-cuffed shirt was unbuttoned low enough to let the chest hair breathe in place of his usual smart necktie.

Within Atlanta's young black jet set, the crowd with which he liked most to be associated, Lance was known for his extravagance. Indeed, he had come to view himself as a kind of master emcee, a Gatsby-like presence whose lavish spending served as a barometer of the times. On his fortieth birthday he had celebrated in South Africa by taking his guests barhopping in a white stretch Mercedes Benz limousine. Here, on his forty-first, the outer rim of the dance floor was lined with tables holding mounds of Gulf shrimp and exotic cheeses, ornate pastries and lavish chocolates, and bottle upon bottle of wine and champagne. The spread, along with the sweet perfume of the women mingling with the scent of roses and lilies, crystallized notions that the man with "L.H.H." monogrammed on his cuff was a player around town. It may have helped, too, to distract from the unsettling truth that Atlanta's gilded age, forged some thirty years prior by the city's black old guard, was coming to an end.

In Atlanta, the black elite was divided into an older generation of insular, tradition-bound natives and a younger, high-living group of nouveau riche transplants. Both groups were obsessively image-conscious, though it was in the latter that Lance had stature, and in which he wanted to continue to amass cachet. Lance had earned his reputation in technology. Access Inc. assisted companies in developing sophisticated information networks, and he had been so successful that *Inc.* magazine had included it among America's Top 500 enterprises. But Lance considered this achievement to be of secondary value. His real prowess, he often boasted, was in the network of relationships he had nurtured and built across town with high-up people at Coca-Cola, Delta Airlines, and Wachovia Bank, for example, and within such professional organizations as the prestigious Leadership Atlanta, and a bundle of others, from the Atlanta Business League to the Atlanta Chamber of Commerce and the Data Processing Management Association. He had become a central figure in the social scene of the city that was the capital of the New South.

To be sure, nobody understood more clearly than Lance the necessity of reaching out to the city's older black establishment—the Jesse Hills and Herman Russells and Coretta Scott Kings—and he had successfully made many of those contacts as well. It was said among Lance's colleagues that his networking of Old Atlanta was genius. He knew how to get what he wanted from that set, even though he was not part of it—not invited to socialize with the Alexanders, the Dobbs, the Scott clique. Admittedly, he was not particularly fond of this crowd, though he felt that he understood them. They were, above all, a proud people. Proud of the fact that their great-great-grandfather was a medical doctor or lawyer or once ran a successful business on Auburn Avenue. Proud that Atlanta was the only city in the world with five black colleges in a central area. Proud that Atlanta was a place where you found fifth-generation college-graduate blacks, unheard of in most other cities. He understood that in Atlanta, it wasn't necessarily money that made you part of that clique. It was heritage.

Lance may have lacked the pedigree of Atlanta's established black bourgeoisie, but he had plenty of drive. In this, he typified the wave of young black strivers who had migrated to Atlanta and other southern cities over the past three decades. Atlanta was the epicenter of this buppie gold rush, as the city's black population had more than doubled during that period. The last time so many blacks packed their bags at once was during the Great Migration of the 1930s to flee the oppression of the South for freedom and factory jobs in Chicago, Detroit, and Cleveland. This time around, the lure of white-collar corporate and government jobs and warmer weather had spurred an epic U-turn that demographers called the "Reverse Migration."

Lance Herndon was known for outworking old and new Atlantas alike. He was the sort who measured the success of his day by how many new avenues he had opened up for himself and others, spending weekday evenings working the cocktail circuit and attending dinners and meetings with his clients in the IT division of some large company, where he was constantly reaching out to this guy and offering him four Braves tickets for Saturday afternoon; or to that lady inquiring about her smart daughter at Yale who might make the perfect summer intern for an attorney friend of his; or scheduling coffee and cocktails and phone conversations in this or that city with what seemed like everyone with a meaningful business card. For years, the result had not only been double-digit growth in revenues at Access, but an ability to call in favors from some of the most prominent leaders across town, straight up to Mayor Bill Campbell.

Tonight's fete, though, was aimed at courting not the city's old

guard but rather what Lance liked to call "the beautiful people"—
his real contemporaries—that crowd of young, fashionable black
professionals, the athletes, entertainers, and entrepreneurs and all
their various groupies who gave Atlanta's nightlife its pulse. They
were his social soul mates, so to speak. They were the high-rolling,
Gucci-wearing cats and their stiletto-heeled women who fancied
the dramatic over the mundane, who on other evenings pulled up to
Atlanta Nights or Mr. Vee's or The Parrot in their chromed-out
Lamborghinis and Aston Martins where hulking nylon-shirted
goons with six-pack abs rushed the car to spirit them into perfume-
scented VIP heaven.

Tucked in Lance's wallet was always a slip of paper folded down
to the size of a Chiclet, listing some three dozen very hot women
and their phone numbers. The list never left his possession. For
years, his Friday-afternoon routine was to dial them up one by one
and tell them to meet him at Atlanta Nights for happy hour. The
draw was always big. Women he had not even invited would show,
and so long as they were easy on the eyes, Lance didn't mind a bit.
It got to a point where at 6:00 P.M. on Friday, women would drive
by Atlanta Nights, and upon spotting Herndon's platinum Lotus—
lately it had been the Porsche—parked in his customary front space
directly under the neon, they would sashay in to eat and drink on
his dime. One of them usually followed him home. Sometimes two.

Tonight, Lance strolled through his soiree and greeted his guests.
A great many of them, as usual, were women. The room went quiet
as all eyes were riveted on a three-tiered, chocolate-frosted birthday
cake that had appeared in the center of the dance floor, its forty-one
candles glowing in the dark like a mini constellation. As Lance
moved through the crowd toward his cake, he looked genuinely
humbled, especially when he was greeted by the lead singer for the
Atlanta-based R & B group Silk, a gifted tenor who riffed melodi-

cally through a Grammy-worthy version of "Happy Birthday." Lance blew out the candles, and applause erupted. Then the deejay went back to work, kicking in with rap trio Salt-N-Pepa's funky hit "Push It."

As the crowd converged onto the dance floor, Lance put his arm around an unfamiliar young woman. A petite size four, fair skin, fine straight hair, she was everything he liked. Redbones, he called them. Jerking his shoulders back and shuffling his feet—Lance loved to dance, even though he had no rhythm—he threw his arms up high, his world cloaked in a kind of weightless, enchanted air. With the music pumping and his guests partying hard, Lance leaned into the creamy cheekbone of his blushing new admirer and whispered something in her ear. He may have mused that life didn't get much better than it was that very moment.

Lance Herndon was born in Harlem on April 4, 1955. His parents, Russell and Jackie, were working-class people a generation removed from a long line of Florida and Virginia farmers. An only child, tiny in physical stature and prone to every manner of childhood ailment, Lance is said to have cried his way through the first couple years of his life. His wailing usually got him his way, as he spent much time in the care of babysitters. His mother clocked as much time as she could as a clerk at J. C. Penney's.

Russell's reputation is that he was neither dependable nor much involved in his son's development. When he wasn't hustling odd jobs like trucking local retail merchandise across the boroughs, Russell ran with a group of barhopping men in Brooklyn who called themselves the Hundred Dollar Club, a loosely knit party frat whose sole requirement for membership was paying a few bucks to the brothers anytime you were caught with less than a hundred dollars in your wallet. "We wore the best suits in town," Russell boasted about his threads in those days. "Man, I stayed in Pee-air Car-deen!"

Jackie and Russell split before their son reached adolescence. With Jackie so busy working—she also regularly played bridge with girlfriends, often late into the night—Lance spent much of his childhood alone at home. By the time he was a teenager, he was accustomed to being governed by babysitters and strict handwritten notes from Jackie on how his time was to be spent. "I was pretty much raised by notes," he would later tell his employees, defending his preference for communicating by notes at the office.

Lance loved his mother, but he worshipped his paternal grandfather, John Harrison Herndon. He would later name his own son after his granddad. John Harrison was a slightly built, deeply religious man who, along with his wife Elver, lived off the land in Farmville, Virginia, an hour west of Richmond. Because of the strain in his parents' marriage, Lance, from the age of seven until thirteen, lived with his paternal grandparents in the small rural town. He attended elementary school by day and helped tend to the cows and chickens and farm tobacco in the late afternoon. A deacon in the local Baptist church, John Harrison warmed to the curious young kid and tried to teach him everything he knew about running a farm. The first lesson, of course, was starting the day early. Granddad and grandson would rise together at dawn, eat breakfast, and begin their duties. In perhaps his first lesson in entrepreneurship, Lance was given a calf by his grandfather, who trusted him to raise it. John Harrison would later take Lance to sell the steer at market, giving the boy cash for his work. Lance was forty years old when John Harrison died. At the funeral, he cried like a baby.

Lance proved to be no more successful at the altar than his parents. He spent his twenties floundering through two brief marriages; first to a pretty Puerto Rican woman, and again to a rather clingy Creole from New Orleans ten years his junior. Neither marriage lasted far beyond the first anniversary. It was while vacationing in Brazil in the early 1990s, that he met his third and final wife, Jeannine Price, a flight attendant for Citibank. By then, he had graduated in computer science from City College of New York and moved to Atlanta to launch Access. The firm, whose specialty was providing staffs of computer technicians to build networks and databases for businesses, had grown quickly to boast such clients as Coca-Cola, Hartsfield International Airport, and NationsBank. He was thirty-five.

Jeannine Price, a native of Kansas City, Missouri, was a refined black woman, a debutante sort and devout Catholic who had invested most of her time throughout high school and during college at the University of Missouri–Kansas City studying ballet. Upon graduating college, she danced with a Kansas City ballet company and had hoped one day to join the Dance Theatre of Harlem, the only black classical company in the nation. But after several knee injuries, she had been forced her to give up her dance career. She became a flight attendant, first in commercial and then corporate. At Citibank, many of her trips were international flights.

Years later, Jeannine would regale friends with the dreamy story of a weeklong trip to Rio, how the atmosphere was festive because of Carnivale, a traveling celebration of Caribbean culture. The city was in full swing, with lots of drinking and dancing, but she was alone, and so she decided to take a tour bus and visit the statue of Christ. The bus climbed Corcovado Mountain and the scenery was magnificent, breathtaking—the Rio de Janeiro skyline and the white beaches along the coast of the city. The place was packed with tourists when she got off the bus, but she eased her way through the crowd until she got to the base of this gigantic statue—Christ the

Redeemer, it is called—and when she looked up, she was in awe. There was Jesus towering over the city with his arms open wide, as though embracing the skyline. It was humbling to stand there in the shadow of this spiritual monument, and she remembered thinking, Here I am, thousands of miles away from home, standing at the base of this majestic statue in this gorgeous country. It's sunny, it's clear, and I wish there was just somebody, anybody, in this sea of people—everyone seemed to be speaking Portuguese—to share this moment with. As Jeannine was thinking this, she heard someone speaking English and the crowd seemed to open up, and there stood this black man. Small, dark brown, with a thick mustache, he made eye contact, came over, and they started a conversation. He said he was over there on vacation with his accountant. She couldn't believe it: suddenly, here she was with this beautiful man. It seemed more like fate than coincidence. "Meeting your man in a foreign country beneath a statue of Jesus," she said. "It just doesn't get much better than that!"

Within a year, in 1990, they were married and building their dream house—a six-thousand-square-foot colonial in the exclusive hilltop community of Northcliff, a wealthy suburban enclave in Roswell, about thirty minutes north of Atlanta. Situated atop rolling green landscape, the Northcliff subdivision ascends from the Chattahoochee River. Their house, 9060 Bluffview Trace, sat secluded behind quiet, narrow streets in a cul-de-sac of lush trees and foliage, its facade of gray stucco and white marble lattice barely visible to neighbors. Inside was a unique trilevel floor plan; the master bedroom, along with the kitchen, living room, and dining area, were set on a hill at ground level while below, with sweeping landscape views, was a large entertainment area and several guest bedrooms. The bottom level was a bright office suite for Access Inc., where Lance's employees worked under his strict guidance.

Jeannine admired her husband's work ethic, even if his management style tended toward extreme. He believed, for instance, that verbal communication with his employees was a waste of precious time. He made it clear to them that he would rather spend his time out meeting with clients or in his office pitching his services to potential ones—"dialing for dollars" as he called it. To limit his workday conversation, Lance adopted a unique management-by-tape-recorder system. At 4:00 A.M. each morning, he would wake up, pad downstairs in his pajamas and slippers, and recite a list of specific instructions into three tape recorders for employees to follow when they arrived for their workday. "Good morning, Holly, this is Lance," the tape would begin. "Today, I need you to . . ." or "Good morning, Zonya. Please call Wachovia Bank and find out . . ." and so on. He would leave the tape recorders on the desks, along with a corresponding assortment of files and memos. At the end of each workday, employees were required to turn in a report listing all the projects they had completed, along with the recorder. There was not a single workday that his employees could not recall a tape awaiting them. A heavy sleeper, Lance made sure he maintained the practice by placing three clocks around his bedroom, each set to go off at ten-minute intervals starting at 3:40 A.M.

Eventually, Jeannine noticed that Lance had stopped communicating with her, too. As a result, she did not live in the house long. Shortly after giving birth to their son, Harrison, she moved out with the infant and filed for divorce. On the morning Lance's body was discovered, he was living there alone.

chapter two

THE FINAL HOURS

Jackie Herndon stood proudly in her dining room and offered a prayer over her home-cooked meal. Jackie's specialty was seafood, and spread across the table in her best dishes was gumbo, crab cakes, fried catfish, and broiled salmon. There was also corn on the cob, black-eyed peas, green beans, tossed salad, peach cobbler, and a tall pitcher of iced tea—all to celebrate the visit of Lance's ninety-two-year-old paternal grandmother, Elver Herndon, who lived in Farmville, Virginia.

Nearly a dozen family members had crowded into Jackie's small apartment that evening because they knew old Elver, the family matriarch, would not live much longer. She was feeble and Alzheimer-stricken, and it was unlikely she would ever be well enough to travel such a distance again. Elver had always doted on Lance, her only grandchild, and had promised him a few years back that she would come and spend a few nights in that big house she had heard so much about. Lance generally dined out in restaurants, and so Jackie took it upon herself to prepare a feast that night and fill her modest apartment with family. As Elver sat quietly on the living room sofa, there was a bittersweet finality to the occasion.

Lance had spent most of the week hanging out at the Olympic Game festivities across the city, but he made time earlier in the day to pick his grandmother up from the airport and show her around his house and neighborhood. Of course, while he considered himself a family man, this was actually not so true in practice; that evening, at around 8:00 P.M., Lance looked at his watch and announced that he had other business to tend to. His ex-wife Jeannine, mother of their now four-year-old son Harrison, offered to drop Elver off at Lance's home later on. Lance was appreciative, and bid her and the rest of his family farewell. It was the last time any of them would see him alive.

My baby!!!
Okay. Where's your baby?
9060 Bluffview Trace.
Okay. Tell me what's going on.
I came in the house. I found him in bed. He's bleeding. Hurry, please!
Okay, what I need to know is what's going on? Why do you think, what do you think happened?
I don't know, he's all bleeding in bed.
Okay, is he breathing?
I don't know, I can't, just come here please!

It was a quarter after eight when Lance stepped down into Access Inc., located in the basement of his home and remodeled into an office suite. If Lance tended toward grandiosity in his social life, he was decidedly frugal in running his business. He had decided years ago, for example, that it was rarely necessary to invite clients to his office. On those occasions when he needed to impress them, he leased temporary space at Perimeter Mall, where he would hang up his Access shingle for a few hours. He estimated that he had surely saved himself millions in overhead this way.

Lacey Banks was sitting at her desk behind a stack of envelopes that night, listening to music on the radio and typing addresses on envelopes for Lance's upcoming party—an August 18 event he was hosting for the Black Data Processors Association at Jazzman's, a posh Midtown club. She stood up to hug Lance and quietly got back to work.

Although she was his mistress, Lacey knew when to act as simply an employee. Lacey technically was not even an Access employee but rather was paid out of Lance's pocket for occasionally taking on small administrative tasks. A sweet-natured North Carolinian who had proven too restless—if not distracted—for college herself, Lacey admired professional drive in others. Lance's tenacity was a source of awe to Lacey. In fact, she considered her association with him to be among her best assets. It did not bother her that she didn't quite measure up to Lance's standard of beauty, as she was certainly attractive enough. She had smooth almond skin, a slender waist rising to an ample bosom. And Lance liked her face, lightly freckled across the bridge of her nose, and those sunny eyes that added a girlishness to her thirty-five years.

———

That evening, Lance asked Lacey whether he had gotten any phone calls. Lacey handed over a few messages, and Lance disappeared into his office. Minutes later, he returned and sat down across from her and asked her to make out an invitation to a woman named Rachel Morris, explaining that he had forgotten to add this new friend to the list. Lacey had proven not the jealous sort, and Lance felt comfortable sharing that Rachel was an elementary school teacher. He had taken Rachel out to dinner a few weeks before, and they had gotten along rather well. He wanted to see her again. Besides, he would be free soon, Lance said, considering that he was ready to break with his other girlfriends, Kathi and Dionne. Lacey agreed that he should dump them both, for Kathi was too snooty and Dionne too pushy.

At around nine, the phone rang. Lance answered and quickly put the call on hold, then went upstairs to speak to the caller. When he returned a few minutes later, his mood seemed to have shifted, Lacey would later tell investigators. Lance's demeanor had become dark, somber. When she asked him whether everything was all right, he told her things were fine and went back upstairs.

Lacey says that she finished the invitations at 10:30 P.M., and as she headed up to say good night—as Lance's frequent lover, Lacey could move freely about the house—Lance was standing in the hallway outside his bedroom with an armful of women's clothing. This struck Lacey as odd, and she asked Lance what he was doing with the clothes. He explained he was moving Kathi's clothes out of his bedroom closet into a hallway closet. Lacey was confused, but didn't press the matter. She was tired and had to awaken early for work the next morning. Lance was constantly scheming, and she would likely learn more about this particular one another time.

Lance walked her to the door and stood in the garage, watching

her as she ran through the pouring rain to her car. Her final image
was of Lance standing beside his Porsche waving good-bye. By
then, it must have been about 10:37 P.M., she would tell police. She
did hear his voice again, later that night. Greeting her when she got
home was a voice message on her answering machine. "Hey, Lacey,
this is Lance," the recording said. "You know, you really ought to
think about marrying me."

She phoned Lance back at around 11:00 P.M., and he picked up.
"You're crazy," she told him. They both laughed. Then she went
to bed.

His head is bashed in? Okay. Do you see anything around
him like a . . .
I see his head bashed in ma'am.
Okay, is there anybody in the house?
I just came in here and this is how I found him.
Okay, I don't want you to touch anything, okay?
I'm not touching anything . . .
Okay, but you don't know if he's breathing?
I just set him to the side. He's just all beat up. Somebody
done this to him. I don't know who . . .

Shortly after eight, on the morning after the Herndon family
dinner, employee Holly Steuber settled behind her desk at Access
Inc. A stoutly built brunette, Holly Steuber was the only white
person on staff. She enjoyed her role as a recruiter for Access, hiring
freelance technicians to develop software, manage databases, and
install computer networks for clients, even if there were moments
when she felt like an outsider. Sometimes, for instance, the office
talk became too relaxed for her taste. "I would be sitting in the

office and somebody would use the 'n' word and I would have to tell them not to do it because it bothered me," Holly says. Lance disapproved of much office chatter of any sort, and once stated as much in a terse memo to his employees. Says Holly of her boss: "He was very formal. He did everything in writing."

Coworker Zonya Adams, a young, fair-complexioned Bermudan, arrived about a half hour after Holly. An affable yet serious-minded woman, Zonya Adams was the office manager and Lance's trusted confidante on most business matters. As Zonya would later recall, upon pulling into the driveway, she noticed that one of the four garage doors—the smallest one on the far left, which usually held the Porsche—was ajar. She didn't have a chance to mention this to Holly before Holly brought to her attention something more unusual: absent from their desks were the audiocassette tapes of work instructions Lance always left for them. In their combined ten years with the firm, Lance had never failed to leave on their desks his personally taped recordings detailing how they should spend their workday.

Holly and Zonya pondered the lapse in routine for a moment. Then Holly stepped into Lance's office, where she noticed something else amiss and called out for Zonya to come witness it: Lance's computer was on, and that day's calendar was up on the screen, but it had no entries in it. This was extraordinary, considering that Lance not only lived according to his calendar appointments but also crammed his itinerary with lists of every place he needed to be, everyone he needed to meet, down to fifteen-minute windows. His calendar was gospel. If it indicated playtime with his son Harrison from twelve o'clock to one, they could be sure Lance was somewhere frolicking with the boy during that very hour. His personal date book contained entries for the next three years.

The women tried to stay calm but could not. Holly told Zonya she had already paged Lance once. Both of them knew, though, that Lance was not likely to respond to Holly's page; she lacked the clout to summon his prompt attention so early in the workday. Zonya decided she had better page Lance herself. To ensure he'd call back, she punched in their secret code for emergencies, adding 0-0-1 as a suffix to the company's private line.

As they waited for a response, Holly also realized the office laptop computer was missing. She wondered aloud whether Lance had let his girlfriend Dionne borrow it, which he had done on occasion. But both Holly and Zonya decided Lance would have forewarned them about this a day or so in advance, as he usually did. Zonya looked in the closet to see whether the laptop case was there. It was.

Now they were getting worried. They were also startled by a wan voice calling down from the top of the staircase. They had forgotten that Lance's visiting grandmother was in the house. Elver Herndon was looking for Lance because she wanted to make a bowl of cereal and couldn't find any of what she was looking for in the kitchen. Employees were prohibited from entering the main quarters of the house without Lance's permission, and so Zonya called out that they were looking for Lance and asked her to be patient for a few minutes.

Zonya paged Lance again, this time adding a 9-1-1 suffix to the company number. A few minutes later, feeling desperate, she phoned Lance's mother, Jackie, who lived a couple blocks away. Jackie Herndon arrived at the office around 10:20 A.M., complaining that on the way in she had noticed the garage door was opened slightly, and that Lance needed to be careful or the squirrels were going to get into the Porsche.

She was also frustrated that Zonya and Holly had been unable to contact Lance. She would find Lance herself. He was probably just sleeping in, she said. Surely the man was exhausted. Every night it seemed he was attending some Olympics party or event or game or match or something. She turned and walked up the steps. Seconds later, Lance's mother screamed.

I'm gonna get 'em. I'm gonna get whoever did this to my baby. Whoev—

I, I understand. I understand. Ma'am, ma'am, it's gonna be okay. We're gonna be out there in a few minutes. Okay?

Where are the cops? Where are the cops?

They're on the way. They're gonna be there in a few minutes. It seems like a long time, but trust me.

In the office downstairs, Zonya and Holly were paralyzed. The ceiling rumbled as Jackie scrambled from room to room. Shrill cries slashed the air. Zonya left Holly and locked herself in the office bathroom. Holly stood at her desk, trying to find some sense in the commotion.

A few minutes later, Zonya reappeared.

"I need you to page Jeannine and tell her that something bad must have happened to Lance!" Zonya yelled. "Tell her to come over here immediately. And call Jacques Albright!" Jacques Albright, a prominent Atlanta surgeon, was Lance's best friend. After calling out instructions, Zonya went cowering back into the bathroom.

He's dead! He's dead!

We're gonna be there in a few minutes. Okay? We'll be there ...

Oh, God, God ...

Okay, we're gonna be there in a few minutes. They should be, you know what? You got your front door open?

I'll open it. I'll open it.

Go open it.

He's dead! My baby's dead! My baby's dead! Oh God, they done killed my baby! They done killed my baby!

chapter three

A long the bank of the Chattahoochee River, a band of police cars was moving swiftly through the damp morning air. At a stone pillar entryway, the vehicles slowed and the sirens went quiet as they whisked into the shaded subdivision of Northcliff. The vehicles have to slow as they pass the security kiosk before ascending a steep slope onto Northcliff's winding streets. Arriving in the shaded cul-de-sac of Bluffview Trace, the cars pulled up in front of the large gray stucco house, and several uniformed officers hustled from their cars to make their way through the leafy grove of shrubs and azaleas surrounding the home.

The house was quiet now. Zonya had come out of the bathroom

and was standing beside Holly when they were startled by a figure in the window. A police officer was pointing his gun at them.

"Freeze!"

The officer rushed in through the office door, frisked them for weapons, and asked who they were and what they were doing in the house. The women explained they worked there, and the officer pointed at two chairs.

"Both of you," he ordered. "Sit here and do not move." The officer slid his pistol into his holster and radioed that workers were in the house. He then disappeared upstairs.

Detective William Anastasio, driving an unmarked Ford Taurus, pulled up along the curb and stepped slowly out into the muggy morning. Anastasio was an amateur bodybuilder with a longish face that looks disproportionate to his stout, muscular frame.

Walking up the driveway, Anastasio passed a pair of officers leaving the house in brisk strides toward their squad car.

"We secure in there yet?" Anastasio asked.

An officer told him that it was safe for him to proceed, that only the paramedics and the victim's mother and grandmother, plus a couple of employees in an office downstairs, were in the house.

With his partner Marty Evans following behind, Anastasio pushed open the heavy oak door. Standing in the white marble vestibule, he looked around at the cold interior, spare and gray like a corporate lobby, with hazy outdoor sun filtering down through skylights in high vaulted ceilings. He turned to Evans.

"Find the victim's mother," he instructed. "She's around here somewhere. She called dispatch."

Evans disappeared around a corner while Anastasio started

walking the slate-gray marble floors, taking note of the modern abstract paintings hanging on white walls. The corridors converged at hard flat angles into rooms as clean and uninhabited as laboratories. This was the home of a bachelor, he surmised, most likely divorced, whose wife had likely walked out and left him without much furniture or decorative flair. Anastasio liked to paint such scenarios in his head, see how many of his assumptions would check out in the end. For sure, this house felt sterile, devoid of warmth. The black lacquer furniture was dust-free and looked unused by its owner. The kitchen, with chilly metallic hues and a glass bowl of uneaten Kellogg's cornflakes on the counter, felt equally uninviting.

Toward the far left, near the entry of the first floor, was a narrow corridor leading to the master bedroom suite. Anastasio moved ahead, carefully stepping around a pager and a few loose coins scattered across the gray carpet. At the room's entrance, he stopped cold at the body in front of him. He took a few steps back and called out for his partner.

"This is fuckin' ugly, man," Anastasio said, breathless. Evans ran over to join him. "Get GBI over here fast, and don't let those assholes send us some rookie!"

Outside the house, a burgundy Audi came screeching from around the corner and stopped at the wooden blockade cops had erected at the foot of the cul-de-sac. The car door opened, and a female driver, attractive and slender and dressed in black spandex athletic gear, sprinted out. It was Jeannine Herndon, and she ran several yards before a Roswell officer took hold of her arm to detain her for questioning. She protested, telling the officers that she was Lance's Herndon's ex-wife, that they had a small son together.

"Please let me through," she pleaded.

Anastasio was interviewing Herndon's mother, Jackie, when they heard the commotion outside. Recognizing Jeannine's frantic voice, Jackie cried, "Somebody's got to tell her."

"I'll handle it," he said softly.

Jeannine Herndon has a way of impressing all that meet her. She has the understated softness of a southern belle, but her accent is unadorned midwestern yet pleasant on the ears. Her face has an old-fashioned prettiness, with large inquisitive eyes and sculpted plum-colored lips; her skin is the color of cinnamon.

Jeannine Herndon followed Anastasio over to his car, and once they were inside, he broke the news to her. She cried hard, at times against his chest, then calmed herself enough to explain that she and Lance had divorced that past January, but had been having problems long before that. She went on to say that some people love each other but are just not meant to be together. She and Lance had finally begun to make peace with that fact.

Anastasio went easy on Jeannine Herndon that morning, but he did mention that he had been down in Lance's office and noticed all the awards and citations, and figured that the man was a real mover and shaker and probably pretty well liked around town. When she equivocated, saying that only in certain circles was he was liked, Anastasio began pressing harder.

"Who can you think of that didn't like him, may have had an ax to grind?" he asked.

Jeannine, somewhat hesitantly, explained that Lance was a very successful, very well connected man, and frankly he didn't try to hide it much; he had worked hard to get where he was in life, and he wasn't going to be slighted by anyone.

She made it clear that the one thing Anastasio *did* need to know was that Lance moved in a lot of circles; he was a socialite and made it his business to know anyone he thought mattered. He could be quite giving, even generous to a fault, but he could also be very arrogant at times and difficult, the type that some people would have preferred not to deal with at all—that is, if they had a choice in the matter.

"Just one more question. Are you currently dating anyone, someone who might have reason to want to harm your ex-husband?" Anastasio asked.

Jeannine told him about Thomas Patterson. She had been seeing him since around April, but they were taking things slow in their relationship. Besides, Thomas is a good man, a kind person, she said. There is absolutely no reason whatsoever that he would have anything against Lance. Never once had he even spoken ill of her ex.

A t 11:27 A.M. Sam House, a crime scene analyst for the Georgia Bureau of Investigation, strode out of his dusty blue pickup. He was wearing cowboy boots, jeans, and a plaid shirt rolled up at the sleeves. Smoking a cigarette, he walked over to the car where Anastasio was taking a statement from Jeannine Herndon. When Anastasio and the woman got out of the car, House shook the detective's hand and reminded the detective to collect prints from her.

Sam House was famous throughout the state law-enforcement community. He was known as a real gumshoe, more comfortable inside yellow police tape than in his own leathery skin. He was also an unassuming southern gentleman. He grew up in small-town Bremen, Georgia, where he mastered bagging quail and pheasant and deer before later turning his hunting talent to criminals. "I tend to get a lot of the big murder cases, even though I don't think a whole lot about how well-known a person is. I approach all my investigations the same. I treat it like it was *me* who got killed, or somebody I care about, and then I work from there.

"By the time I got over to Mr. Herndon's house, it had already been secured, and I remember hoping that the scene hadn't been contaminated. I like to be first whenever I can, so that way I can preserve things as they were. In this case, I think I arrived about a half-hour or so after they got started."

Sam House asserted his control quickly that morning, with a battery of questions that Anastasio couldn't really answer. Instead, the detective described the crime scene to House: how the victim was found lying on his waterbed, wrapped in a sheet with his head bashed in. Apparently, he was some big-shot computer guy, a black fellow, and it was clear that somebody had beaten the living crap out of him. Anastasio could not tell House what weapon was used. His guys were still looking for it. Whoever the perp was, there was no sign of forced entry. There were also no significant witnesses yet. He had started questioning the mother, the grandmother, and a couple of women who worked in the house in an office downstairs.

Anastasio followed Sam House as he walked up the driveway. House's sharp eyes scanned the ground for evidence. He paused at the four-car garage. One of its doors was open several inches off the pavement. House peered inside to find a silver Jaguar, a blue Porsche, and a tan Volvo. He stepped over to the partly open roll-up door, pulling a plastic Ziploc bag from his back pocket. He leaned over, picked up a gum wrapper from the pavement, and dropped it in the plastic bag.

By noon that day, the scope of Lance Herndon's influence had become evident as word circulated back to Anastasio that the White House—the caller was actually a close friend of Lance's who had recently joined the Clinton administration's communications staff—had offered to send in FBI agents for support. Police Chief Edwin Williams had politely declined. Anastasio wasn't sure how news of Herndon's death had leaked so quickly. Vans toting camera crews were camped out at the foot of the cul-de-sac, with television reporters posing for live shots and print journalists scribbling in notebooks and barking their sketchy details into cell phones.

Detective Anastasio followed Special Agent Sam House into Lance Herndon's bedroom suite. Along a wall a few feet left of the bed was a wooden chest of drawers, its surface cluttered. There were two VIP Olympics tags, a black sports wristwatch, a black leather wallet, several credit cards, an unopened pack of Trojan condoms, ChapStick, a cigar, a shot-sized bottle of Courvoisier cognac, a bottle of body oil, a can of air freshener, several paper clips, rubber bands, and a few loose coins. And a framed photograph, lying facedown.

Sam House took out a handkerchief and picked up the photograph on the chest of drawers. It was of an attractive fair-skinned brunette posing seductively in a white satin teddy. The men exchanged amused frat-boy glances, and then House remarked how odd it was that this hottie's picture was turned down.

A few feet over, facing the bed, was a large-screen television and VCR. The television was off, while the VCR was in a power-on position, though not playing. Inside its cartridge receiver was an erotic video. On the nightstand was another porn tape, an orgy of black couples featured on its casing.

When House eased back the blood-soaked bedsheet, both men winced and stared a moment before stepping forward. Beneath them, lying on his back, arms folded serenely across his chest, was the victim, his face savagely beaten. The forehead was split open so that the bones and tissue were exposed. The eye sockets, too, were caved in, and shattered bone jutted through the flesh. Beneath the victim's bludgeoned face and the shards of bone sprinkled around his head like a halo was a pool of dried blood on rose-colored sheets. House leaned over to examine the victim's arms and legs, noting a lack of visible defensive wounds.

"This guy was ambushed," House said. "He clearly had no idea what was coming."

The victim appeared to have taken at least a dozen blows to his head, forceful blows delivered with a blunt heavy object. House figured straightaway that whoever did this was no burglar. On the other side of the room, French doors opened onto a deck that was three stories high above the ground. The only way onto the deck was through the bedroom door, which House had just walked through. In securing the scene, investigators had photographed what appeared to be shoe impressions, honeycomb in pattern, coming through that door.

This murder struck House as an act of sheer rage, a personal statement. It was likely that the victim knew his killer, and knew him well. House and Anastasio agreed that the fact that Herndon was covered in his sheets when his mother found him also seemed to suggest a killing of a personal nature, that the murderer probably could not stand the sight of what he had done. Then there were the three clocks; the one on the tall chest of drawers against the north wall, the other on a dresser along the room's east wall, and another on this nightstand, all unplugged. Whoever killed him must have stayed around long enough to worry that those alarm clocks might sound.

Above the victim and headboard, rising up the white walls and ceiling in a V-shaped pattern, was blood spatter, a thick crimson color at the bottom and fainter toward the ceiling. To Sam House, this seemed to indicate that the killer was on top of the victim, straddling him as the weapon repeatedly descended on his head. The darker spatter was the weapon coming up off the skull with fresh blood on it, and the lighter spatter marked the downward arc as it descended for another blow. What this theory didn't explain, though, was the wide fleshy gash at the back crown of Lance Herndon's head. If the assailant was straddling the victim and clubbing his face, then what explained the wound on the back of his head?

Sam House ventured a couple of scenarios on this: the first was that because the victim was killed on a waterbed, there would have been some rocking and swaying each time the killer swung the weapon back to deliver the next blow. The waves might have caused the victim's head to go upright once or twice during the beating. House's other explanation was simpler. The victim might have started from an upright position, perhaps sitting on the edge of the bed, and been caught unsuspecting when the first blow came crashing down on top of his skull. He then fell over on his back, and the killer straddled him to deliver the shower of blows that followed.

Anastasio followed Sam House into the bathroom, and House pointed to the toilet bowl, in which a bloody pillowcase lay soaked in water. Again, House had a ready explanation. After the bludgeoning, the killer wiped off with the pillowcase and tossed it in the commode.

At 3:15 P.M. that afternoon, Lance Herndon's body was placed in a body bag with sheets and liner pad and transported to the Fulton County Medical Examiner for an autopsy. Lance Herndon became homicide case #96–1399.

chapter four

GONE TOO SOON

Shortly after studying the crime scene with Sam House, Detective Anastasio asked the women at Lance's home to follow him to the police station for fingerprinting. Holly drove alone in her car, while Jeannine left her car parked along the curb and rode in Zonya's car. When Lance's mother, Jackie, came out of the house with his grandmother Elver, her arms were flailing.

Staggering toward Anastasio's unmarked car, she yelled up the driveway to Jeannine, "It was those damn women! It was those damn women!"

Later that afternoon, Jeannine and Zonya were numb as they drove back from the station after being fingerprinted. Meanwhile, a media frenzy had taken hold on Bluffview Trace. When Zonya pulled onto the street to drop Jeannine off at her car, reporters were swarming the scene. There were satellite trucks and flashing cameras and microphones all around. Zonya and Jeannine came up with a plan: to avoid the reporters, Zonya would speed up to Jeannine's car, and Jeannine would hop out and speed off in hers without saying a word to anyone.

Y ou sittin' down, Russell?"
     "I was just laying here, snoozing. Why?"
"Lance . . . Lance."
"Yeah, what about him?"

Russell Herndon lives alone in Farmville. That afternoon, a few hours after Jackie had discovered their son's body, Russell had been startled upright when the phone rang. On the line was his cousin Verna from New York. He knew Verna wasn't sounding right. Then she told him.

"They found him this morning, Russell. I'm so sorry. He's dead. Lance is dead."

Russell Herndon saw his son's face as though it was in front of him. For a moment he sat there hoping his hearing had failed him, and that Verna was referring to some other Lance. But he knew somehow, and his creaky old knees sprung him off the sofa. "You're lying to me, Verna! Tell me you're lying, please!"

Verna wept hard. Russell Herndon has never been a religious man, but he fell back and cried out. "Jesus, Lord! Not my boy! What's happened to my boy!"

There was a long silence, and Russell filled it with old fears. He thought of the plane, the single-engine Cessna Lance loved to fly. He thought about how Lance, a few weeks before on his way back home to Atlanta after visiting Farmville, had flown directly above the farmhouse, wobbling the plane's wings back and forth in a kind of saluting motion good-bye. Russell was not at all amused by the stunt, and now he braced himself for word that Lance had died in a plane crash.

"Jackie found him in bed this morning all beaten up," Verna said. "We don't know what happened."

Her words yanked Russell Herndon's thoughts out of the wild sky and focused them back on earth, on the big house Lance built a few years ago in the white suburb of Roswell. Russell had cautioned his son against building such a large home, reminding him that only foolish black folks flaunt their wealth in front of whites. Russell was of a generation who believed that blacks fortunate enough to have something in life ought to be smart enough to hide it from the enemy.

"Tell me," Russell asked, "where was Mama when they found him?"

"She was there in the house," Verna said. "And she ain't doin' too well after, neither. We're all praying Elver can make it through this."

Russell Herndon says he drank himself to sleep that night, and awoke in a cold sweat before the sun rose. He wanted to call Jackie, his ex-wife, but instead reached beneath his bed and slid out a shoebox full of photos. Thumbing through the stack, he paused at a picture of Lance standing behind Jeannine in the foyer of their home during their marriage, his arms wrapped around her waist. He studied a few baby pictures of his grandson Harrison, and even came across one of himself and Jackie standing on the porch in Brooklyn before their split.

There is a picture that was snapped in Brooklyn on a spring night in 1973 after Lance's high school graduation. For the era, Lance is dressed quite fashionably; he is sporting bell-bottomed knit slacks, a psychedelic silk shirt, and clunky platform shoes. His afro is a full moon. It is his expression, though, that is so memorable, that makes you want to hold it and look at it for a while; it shows the sweet, shy smile of a young man, or rather a boy, heading off into the world, his spaghetti-thin frame posed against the sofa. That graduation night Russell sat with Lance and told him how proud he was to have a son who had graduated with honors. "Thank you, Daddy," he recalls Lance saying. "But you haven't seen anything yet. Just give me some time—I'm going places. You'll see. I'm gonna be a millionaire."

On the evening Lance Herndon's body was discovered, Lance's best friend, Dr. Jacques Albright, went to the country morgue and saw Lance, his face maimed almost beyond recognition. That night, he called Zonya, weeping, and told her the funeral would need to be closed-casket. Jacques also met up with mother Jackie Herndon at her apartment. Jackie asked him to assume the role of family spokesman, fielding calls from the press and speaking to family and friends who had heard the news. He was also asked to deal with the many women jockeying with calls and visits to assume a place among the mourning family.

As it turned out, running interference with Lance's women was a complicated assignment. There were women calling and dropping by with food and flowers and condolences at all times of day and night.

Over the next couple of days, with Lance's various women trying to assert their importance in Lance's life, Jacques Albright decided that the family should hold a public memorial on Monday, and then on Tuesday a private funeral for family and close friends only. It was also decided that Lance would be buried in his favorite tuxedo—the black double-breasted with wide satin lapels. It was the tuxedo he had worn a couple of years before during the Entrepreneur of the Year ceremony at the White House.

Jackie also concluded that while Lance may have lived and worked out in Roswell, his funeral should take place in the heart of Atlanta, or more specifically on the hallowed grounds of the Atlanta University Center. Lance would have wanted it that way: he had great respect for those black institutions. Once, upon hearing about the trials of a bright Morehouse student who during his senior year faced expulsion because of debts to the college, Lance met with the young man and offered to pay his debts and tuition that semester. "I want you to pay me back through community service," Lance told the kid. "Do it, or I'll haunt you."

While Lance himself was not an alumnus of any of the AU Center's five historically black colleges, his mother wanted the status of having him eulogized in such a renowned academic setting. The crown jewel of black higher education, the AU Center boasts Morehouse School of Medicine, Morehouse College, Spelman College, Interdenominational Theological Center, Clark Atlanta University, and Morris Brown College over a few square miles. Name a black luminary—whether it's Martin Luther King Jr. or Marian Wright Edelman or even Spike Lee—and it's a safe bet that the AU has played a role in his or her academic development, either directly or by affiliation.

Of course, it has been decades since the AU Center, located on the southwestern edge of downtown, or the West End, as it is known, was known for its aesthetic beauty. The area is as blighted as the grittiest pocket of any major city up north, riddled with vacant lots, boarded-up storefronts, and crumbling houses. To be sure, there are some vestiges of old grandness in the decaying Victorians, with their ornate gingerbread and dental molding with rafter tails and colorful wood siding, in the pretentiously high ceilings, decorative fireplace mantels, and iron fencing. Tourists now and then make their way over to Wren's Nest, the quaint home of scribe Joel

Chandler Harris, author of the beloved Uncle Remus tales, and the Hammond House, an antebellum home built in the early-twentieth-century heyday, when black businesses in the area were thriving. Today, mostly nail salons, chicken shacks, and liquor stores line streets that have been all but forsaken by recent generations of black achievers. Yet despite the neighborhood's distress, Jackie insisted that her son be memorialized in the prestigious AU complex.

On Monday, August 12, 1996, at 10:30 A.M. Lance Harrison Herndon's memorial was held at Martin Luther King Jr. International Chapel on the tree-lined campus of Morehouse College. The chapel was packed that morning as Lance's friends and contacts from the corporate world, community groups, foundations, and various professional organizations, as well as the social scene, came to pay their final respects. There was no casket on display, but rather dozens of photographs celebrating his life. Atlanta mayor Bill Campbell looked weary as he addressed the gathering. "Losing Lance is a tragedy on so many levels that it's hard to find the words to express it," the mayor said.

Bill Campbell was a prickly sort, but he had always been quite fond of Lance. Lance had recognized Campbell's promise back when Campbell, at the age of twenty-eight, campaigned for city council. He won that seat and went on to claim the mayor's office in 1992. During Campbell's first term, Access had been awarded hundreds of thousand of dollars in city contracts.

Lance saw in the mayor a kind of kindred spirit; both men viewed themselves as outsiders to Atlanta's black establishment. Beneath Bill Campbell's preppy, polished veneer—he was educated at Duke University and Vanderbilt Law School—beat the heart of a rebel. He started fighting young. Back in the fall of 1960, amid death threats by the Ku Klux Klan, the seven-year-old Campbell had been sent by his parents to integrate the all-white public school system in Raleigh, North Carolina—alone. The moment is memorialized in a now-famous newspaper photograph of a lanky second-grader holding his mother's hand as he walks home from school past a row of glaring white parents and children. Some thirty black parents had planned to send their children to Murphey Public School that day, but the death threats caused them to back out. Instead, Campbell, a fair-skinned kid in a plaid shirt and short pants, integrated the school solo that morning, and for the next five years he would be punched, kicked, spat on, and humiliated for sport. Even as mayor, Campbell seemed to simmer with distrust for all but a few longtime loyalists. He considered Lance among the trustworthy.

The Reverend Emmanuel McCall performed a moving eulogy about the deeds one performs before heading into the afterlife. Zonya's husband Gary Jenkins sang a mournful ballad by Michael Jackson that morning.

Like a sunset dying
With the rising of the moon
Gone too soon, gone too soon.

After the memorial, Lance's mistress, Lacey, walked over to Zonya. "Here," she said, handing over a Visa card. Lacey explained that Lance had given the credit card to her a couple of years ago for her personal use. "I don't know what I should do with this," she said.

The funeral was held the following day. It was a decidedly more exclusive affair, if only to spare the family any awkwardness caused by Lance's many grieving mistresses, past and present. Jacques Albright had taken it upon himself to hire a security guard to stand at the entrance of Seller's Funeral Home, located near the AU Center. Jacques had instructed the guard to turn away anyone whose name was not on the family's list of invitees. A couple of Lance's women showed up anyway and were denied entry. Lacey Banks stayed home, though she resented being excluded. "It hurt bad not to be there," she says. "I mean, I was closer to him than practically anyone. He was my best friend, really."

Among those selected to attend was Kathi Collins. Dressed in the black of a grieving widow, Kathi arrived with a small entourage who tended to her as she wept loudly down the aisle upon entering. When a pallbearer stepped over to quietly inform her that she would not be sitting with the family, pointing up to the "public" section in the balcony, Kathi's sobbing stopped abruptly. She was peeved—after all, she shared Lance's bed most nights. Everyone knew they were dating. It had been hurtful enough not to be invited to ride in the family limousine, but the dismissal to the balcony was humiliating. Jacques sympathized with her—he felt bad for all of Lance's women, really—but he was trying his best to ensure that his best friend left this world with a measure of dignity, part of which meant keeping them at bay.

Ex-wife Jeannine sat in the front row beside Harrison, along with Lance's four-year-old son. Like his father, Harrison was already displaying a love for aviation. Printed on the funeral program were a few squiggly lines that resembled a spaceship. Beneath the boy's artwork were a few simple words: "My dad and I played Legos and cooked donuts. Then we ate them. They were good."

After the memorial, Zonya had her husband, Gary, drive her over to Fidelity Bank so she could attend to some pressing Access business. She needed to check the balance on Lance's business ac-

count and begin paying off some of the firm's bills. But upon re-
viewing the account, a bank teller issued some surprising news: the
account was empty. Zonya refused to believe this. She was sure that
the bank had made a mistake, and insisted that Lance likely had sev-
eral thousand dollars in the account. The teller spent the next few
minutes double-checking, upon which she admitted an error. Actu-
ally, she said, the account is overdrawn by twelve dollars.

A week after Herndon's corpse was discovered, Detective Anas-
tasio sat in a large air-conditioned office at the Georgia Bureau
of Investigation. Across from him was Dr. Kris Sperry, the state's
chief medical examiner. Pony-tailed with a walrus mustache, Sperry
is an eccentric man, known in his spare time to collect rare comic
books, attend mummy conventions, and jam to the Grateful Dead.
His office, tucked away in downtown Atlanta in an old brick low-
rise called the Stivers Scientific Building, was lined with hundreds
of books covering everything from blood pattern analysis to body
art to antiquarian forensic medicine. These volumes were inter-
spersed with dozens of Tibetan skulls and various human and
animal bones, along with an assortment of plush Beanie Babies.

In the early afternoon of August 12, 1996, on Dr. Sperry's desk
beside a monkey skull filled with M&Ms, was a thick folder labeled
"96-1399." Dr. Sperry flipped the folder open to the stack of photo-
graphs from the crime scene. The hair and blood samples had not
yet made it back from the lab, but he figured it would be helpful to
share what could be surmised thus far from Lance Herndon's au-
topsy, particularly considering that Anastasio was investigating the
case without benefit of significant physical evidence.

To be sure, stress had been rising over the past week. The dis-
covery of Lance Herndon's corpse had set off a mild panic that

started at the Fulton County District Attorney's Office and had
worked its way down to every branch of local law enforcement.
The mood among Atlanta's brass was already dour. Days earlier, as
the city hosted the Olympic Games, a shrapnel-laden pipe bomb
had exploded during a music concert in Centennial Olympic Park,
killing a woman and wounding nearly a hundred others. There was
still no arrest.

While hardly as big as the Olympic bomber case had become,
the Herndon investigation came with its own worries for city offi-
cials. It was already clear that Herndon had friends in high places.
Mayor Bill Campbell, generally criticized for being aloof about
matters not involving downtown redevelopment, had canceled a
trip so that he could attend Herndon's funeral.

Anastasio understood the politics at work in the Lance Herndon
case. The unsolved murder of a black businessman in Atlanta, a city
whose national image was spun as a black mecca, was simply bad
PR. Anastasio was slowly becoming its scapegoat. Fulton County
DA Paul Howard, newly elected and the first black to assume
the post—and incidentally a close acquaintance of Herndon's—
was phoning Anastasio's boss regularly, and made no effort to
conceal his disappointment in the department's lack of workable
leads. The *Atlanta Journal-Constitution*, too, had become fixated
on the murder, and Anastasio's role as lead investigator of the well-
publicized case had sparked some jealousy among his colleagues.
When Anastasio sat down with Sperry, the chief medical examiner,
that afternoon, he was mentally exhausted and grateful for any nug-
gets Sperry might have to offer.

Anastasio asked Dr. Sperry what could be learned thus far from
the autopsy. Sperry began by telling the detective that the actual
cause of death was crushing head injuries. He pointed to the photo-
graph and to three groupings of blunt-force injuries to the victim's

head. Sperry's index finger traced the image of Herndon's bloody skull in the photo. The one at the back of the head, he said, was a single laceration, a straight line about an inch and a half in length. This blow appeared to have come at an angle from left to right, Sperry explained. Accounting for the fact that sequencing injuries is hardly an exact science, Sperry said he believed the blow to the upper back of the head was, in fact, the first.

This back-of-the-head injury, in and of itself, was not particularly serious, Sperry continued. In fact, he doubted that this blow alone would have been fatal or even strong enough to render Herndon unconscious. More likely, it made him dazed and disoriented for a short time.

Still, Sperry believed that this confusing wound came first because it was the only injury back there. He figured Herndon might have been in the process of turning around, which meant the next part of his head exposed was likely the right temple area. There were certainly a few blows right there—not too many, maybe three or four. Still, it was probably the blow to the back of the head, coupled with those to the right temple, that rendered him unconscious.

So then, what actually killed him? Anastasio asked. Sperry responded by sliding out another Polaroid to reveal a full view of Herndon's mangled face. With the victim unconscious and lying on his back, Sperry said, his assailant began hammering his face. The bones in his face were crushed like an eggshell. They were pulverized over and again. As the scalp and soft facial tissues were driven against the bones inside, the jagged edges ripped through the skin.

The front of his face caved in, Sperry went on. Basically, all the bones in the front of the face—the eyebrows, the bones of the nose, the cheekbones on each side, which also comprise the orbits where the eyes sit—were broken. The right side of the jaw, and the upper jaw—all these bones of the central face—were shattered.

Detective Anastasio asked whether Sperry could determine the weapon used to kill Herndon. Sperry admitted that he was at a loss to guess at a probable weapon, except that the instrument likely had a broad or slightly rounded surface with a curved edge of some sort, and must have been solid and heavy to cause this kind of damage. He noted that the frontal bone going across the top of the skull, or rather the victim's entire forehead, was broken into multiple fragments, and pieces of bone were driven into the brain. Only something quite heavy with a lot of power behind it could cause such damage. Sperry estimated that the victim suffered a minimum of eleven blows, but probably more like fourteen or fifteen.

As Sperry finished explaining his theories regarding a probable time of death, Anastasio put forth one final question: Based on the severe injuries and the strength required to cause them, was it plausible that a woman killed Lance Herndon?

Dr. Sperry was clear in his answer: this was entirely possible. To generate the force needed to cause such injury, the same principles of physics are at work as in swinging a golf club. Assuming that her upper body and arm strength were not impaired by polio or another debilitating illness, Sperry said, there was absolutely no reason to believe that a woman could not have murdered Lance Herndon.

chapter five

BLACK MECCA

One of Lance's neighbors, a straight-laced, worldly sort named Ken Crooks, has fond recollections of his early days getting to know Lance. Crooks would eventually ascend to vice president of a major telecommunications company, but back in the mid-1980s he was working as a financial consultant. He met Lance upon relocating to Atlanta from New Jersey with his wife and two daughters. Crooks recalls Lance as a generous man who was eager to share his business and social contacts with his new black neighbor.

The first time Crooks met Lance, Jeannine was still pregnant with Harrison. She came down to the house and welcomed Crooks into the neighborhood. About an hour later Lance stopped by. He was driving a Lotus Elan, a European sports car that, even back then, was priced close to six figures. "He came into my life as a kind of family man, but with a lot of style," Crooks says. "He was quite unassuming at first, claiming that he ran a *little* business. And he really took to my kids."

Crooks and Lance rarely saw each other in the neighborhood. But then on one occasion, Lance invited Crooks out. They met up with Jacques Albright. As it turned out, Jacques and Crooks knew each other from the black ski summit each year. Crooks had been skiing in the New York club, and Jacques was in the Atlanta club. The fact that Crooks already knew Jacques created a kind of instant bond between Lance and Crooks. Lance did not let people into his world easily; he was gracious and gentlemanly, but closed off in other ways.

In the early days of their friendship, Lance began introducing Ken Crooks to *his* Atlanta, a city teeming with ambitious blacks who had relocated there from across the country. Successful blacks in town were the rule, not the exception. It was commonly understood that if you were black and had anything on the ball—some initiative, intellect, skills—if you couldn't make it in Atlanta, you could not make it anywhere. This was a city where black people prospered; where chic brothers and sisters handed off the keys of their expensive foreign sedans to valets at Lenox Mall as they set off for afternoon spending sprees in the designer boutiques; chatted over mimosas at the Buckhead Ritz-Carlton, adorned in silk and linen; sipped wine at poolside later that evening in the big homes of Alpharetta; and preened with barely contained gusto at church on Sunday mornings, a phalanx of fashion-forward Christians getting the Holy Ghost in the pews of chapels the size of Gothic cathedrals.

Ken Crooks took in the social scene, but he was more impressed by Lance's professional side, the great lengths Lance went to nurture his business relationships. Lance, for instance, once took a group of business clients down to a naval base on the Florida-Georgia border where he treated them to an overnight cruise on a submarine, courtesy of an admiral friend he had made during a visit to the White House. Years later, his guests were still overwhelmed. "Just being invited was mind-blowing," gushed Dan Owens, a middle-aged white guy who went on the trip. "I was thinking the only thing bigger than this might be getting shot into space on a shuttle. We got down there on a Saturday morning, and we had a very nice little luncheon with the commanding officer, who welcomed us and gave us a little briefing on the submarine, and then he took us on. The only thing I can compare it to is the starship *Enterprise*. It was ten stories high, and couple of football fields in length, just incredible. The thing has got like fifty thousand horsepower and a tank so big you don't have to refuel for twenty years. You can cruise at such high speeds you can be anywhere in the world in a day or two. They make their own water, air, and electricity. And the food is wonderful; the chefs have studied at the finest French culinary schools. I'm in my bunk and I can't even sleep, thinking, Wow, I am in a submarine. It was a fantasy. What an experience Lance gave me."

As a newcomer, Ken Crooks also admired Lance's tenacity in making his mark in a city that, based on Crooks's few months living there, seemed clubby and provincial—particularly the black community. "It was kind of like if you weren't an Atlanta native or you didn't go to Spelman or Morehouse, you were told to go step over there somewhere, you weren't allowed to come inside this wall. I had gone down there thinking it was a black mecca, and I was enthusiastic. But it occurred to me that all the people who were doing all the fundraising for Campbell when he was running for mayor were native Atlantans. All the educated blacks moving down there for corporate jobs were moving outside of Atlanta into the surrounding counties.

"In the Northcliff subdivision where we lived, there were about two hundred homes and six black families. If you compare that to other subdivisions around, most of the others also had just a sprinkling of blacks who really didn't know each other and really didn't know Atlanta. So you really don't create a power base that way. Everyone is on the periphery looking in. If you really wanted to know the folks who were doing things, they were usually the folks living downtown in the older homes, like in Cascade Heights, where everybody knew everybody. It was like a pattern: you could almost see the real estate agents sending people out of downtown Atlanta into the suburbs."

The result was such exclusive addresses as Sandstone Shores and Sandstone Estates, all-black lake communities of sprawling brick and stucco mini-mansions set dramatically against wooded lots and groves of pine trees. Rich in architectural splendor, these homes, with their stone pillar entrances decorated with massive lion heads and pyramids, are required by code to have at least nine thousand square feet of custom-built living space, enough to house indoor pools and gymnasiums and theaters. The Sandstones were built in the boom of the 1980s and by the mid-1990s were marketed to the young and affluent, such as R & B singer Kelly Price, whose regal stucco home looms castle-like behind a wrought-iron entrance and freshly manicured shrubs. From the street you can hear the soft babble of the stone fountain on the front lawn. Through the home's arching picture window, you can see broad white pillars and several balconies and staircases swirling down to the blue waters of an aquarium in an atrium.

The suburban migration had the effect of further isolating middle-class blacks. "Lance had moved to Atlanta about fifte

years before, and I think he was just annoyed that there were na-
tives or more established families who thought they were in the
know and kept others locked out. I think that Lance thought a lot
of people, especially the old Atlanta crowd, were full of shit because
they felt like they should be only ones in the know."

Lance, for instance, never forgave the wealthy black owner of a
large local construction company—a solid member of the city's old
guard—for disrespecting him one night. One of Lance's business
associates had arranged for Lance to have dinner at the man's home,
yet Lance found himself waiting for more than an hour before his
host finally appeared—dressed in pajamas. Years later, Lance would
recall to friends how the old tycoon sat aloofly and ate his food
without uttering a word to Lance before disappearing back upstairs.
That dismissal was a turning point in Lance's perception of Atlan-
ta's old black money.

Of course, Lance was far too practical to abandon courting the
city's important black establishment altogether, but he preferred to
work alternate routes to get whatever he needed. "Lance repre-
sented a guy who walked both lines," Crooks said. "He gave money
to Campbell, and so a lot of the political folks knew him. And cor-
porate folks knew him, too, especially over at NationsBank. There
weren't a whole lot of black entrepreneurs who had legions of
people on their payroll as consultants. And the one thing about
Lance was that he was a results-oriented guy. If Lance said he was
going to get you the weather report on Tuesday, you would have
the weather report on Tuesday. And there were just a lot of people
in Atlanta that Lance felt didn't put their money where their mouth
was because they never delivered on stuff like that. His strength
was pretty simple: in business, if you keep your word, people are
going to do business with you. He was determined to build a suc-
cessful business, and he did."

Lance was also convinced that his social image needed to match his professional one. By the time he started hanging out with Ken Crooks, Lance had pushed away several old friends, notably a fellow named Len, a local graphic artist from Augusta, and Rudy, a streetwise classmate from back at Westinghouse High School. Rudy was a brooding creative type unwilling to compromise himself for crass commercial gain, preferring to live frugally on drywalling and housepainting projects while struggling to sell his hip neon master-pieces on consignment at funky art houses. Rudy had moved to At-lanta with his wife and their yapping miniature terriers Abbott and Costello after serving several years in the army. Lance was fond of both Len and Rudy, though he considered Rudy his most trusted confidant. In fact, he and Rudy had been so close that in the early stages of dating Jeannine, he impressed upon her only half-jokingly that she needed to pass Rudy's scrutiny before things could get really serious between them. As Lance became more popular on the social scene, he gradually withdrew from both Len and Rudy, be-lieving these old friends lacked the proper level of style and sophis-tication to fit into his new world. He filled the slot with Jacques Albright, whose thriving medical practice enabled him to afford a high-end nightlife and the spontaneous getaways out of the country that had become routine recreation for Lance.

Around the time that Lance began to seriously befriend Ken Crooks, Lance had begun losing interest in his marriage to Jeannine as well, although Ken Crooks did not learn this until much later in their friendship. Lance's home life had become uninspired. Jeannine bored him, he confided to his closest female friends. He vented his frustration in biting critiques of her appearance. Lance had said some hurtful things before they married: he once, for instance, had commented on her complexion, saying that she was lucky because he wasn't generally attracted to "dark" women, and she was the darkest woman he had ever dated. While Lance's prejudice stung, Jeannine discarded it as male nonsense instead of a glimpse into the deep-seated issue he had with his own dark brown skin tone. "Lance's women all look the same," his father Russell said. "Redbones, that's all he liked."

In marriage, though, Lance's jabs extended to his wife's clothes. He told Jeannine that she possessed no sense of style, that her clothes were dull, matronly, and he often scolded her to "pump up" her outfit on those occasions when he did take her out, which were becoming less frequent. Jeannine did modernize her wardrobe and started wearing trendier, skimpier outfits. At his urging, she even switched to a high-end salon that gave her a sassy new short cut. But Lance was never quite satisfied, and by the time Jeannine became pregnant in the spring of 1991, he seemed to prefer going out alone.

"I think Lance allowed me into his personal world because of my rapport with Jacques and because I basically kept my mouth shut," Crooks says. "We would go out and he would have these women and I wouldn't say a thing and so I guess he felt like, 'Ken's cool. He'll help watch my back.' And let's face it—a lot of women took to Lance because he was charming. He was always well dressed. His clothes always fell just right. His hair was always cut. He was very detail-oriented about keeping himself right. But he also had this ability to—and this was the one thing that made me afraid for him—he had the ability to use people. He could shut these women down at the drop of a pin. Somewhere along the way he had learned how to do that. He would just start feeling as though some woman he was seeing had been the flavor last month but no more, and he'd lose interest. Just that quick. And he didn't have a lot of trouble telling them that.

"He could get away with being dismissive like that. On top of the charm, there was his reputation of being a young millionaire. I mean, what was communicated to me early on, in a first impression, was not only the Elan, but he also had two other cars in the garage, a Benz and a Jag. He had custom-built his home, and when you went into it you could tell someone spent a lot of time going through the architectural details and decorating. Everything was put in place and planned, everything was landscaped nicely. And then when you got him talking about his business, you would hear about all the consultants working here and there for him; like I said, I knew he had a contract with NationsBank, and so I'm thinking he's got a cash-flow machine. I'm thinking that after profits, he's probably keeping ten or fifteen percent of whatever he's making, and back then he was probably billing a couple million dollars in revenue. And me, with an understanding of finance and operations, I figured he was probably taking in four or five hundred thousand dollars a year, which wasn't bad at all back then.

"But I also noticed that he was spending a lot of it. He liked to eat out a lot. He liked to pick up the check. He was very generous socially to kind of demonstrate, you know, his wealth. But some of the things he'd say now and then made me start realizing that something might be wrong. He'd say things like, I just got my American Express bill, and it's twenty-five thousand dollars. Or he'd say, I got my rate down to four percent, and I knew he'd probably done that because he needed cash. I never said anything, though. When I heard that he was having a cash-flow problem, I looked back and saw the indicators. He was using cash flow from his business to pay all his monthly recurring stuff and using the interest rate differential to pull out cash. So I knew he was playing pretty hard.

"In the end, I stopped hanging out with him so much. He had taken part ownership in a nightclub called The Vixen. He and Jeannine had broken up, and I was still married, so my relationship with him changed because of that. He was hanging out pretty hard and throwing these Lacey parties. I never wanted to do those. Lacey Banks was a plaything for Lance. He would take her to clubs or meet her at them, and she'd show up wearing a really short skirt or one with a slit up the leg. She was a showpiece. I remember once when he was picking up a new Mercedes, she was there waiting at the dealership for him in a well-fitting dress. I thought she worked for him. And he shared some stuff with me in the car later. He explained that he had money and that Lacey liked to roll with men who had money. I took it to mean that, while she had a pretty body, she wasn't very bright."

Aside from women, Herndon's favorite escape had become flying. He flew a single-engine Cessna, and he loved pushing it to the limits. Yet even this hobby had begun to leave him wanting. Toward the end of his life, Herndon had developed a friendship with a flight instructor and paid him for lessons in performing spins in his airplane. A dangerous, daredevil flight maneuver, spins were long ago a required training regimen for new pilots, but were banned by the FAA around mid-century. Most aircraft these days are designed to resist spinning, but Lance pressed his instructor for a lesson. Spinning gave him the thrill of his life. Thousands of feet in the air, Lance peered down through the window as the plane headed straight down at the world, spinning and spinning out of control.

chapter six

FAIR GAME

On the night of his forty-first birthday bash, Lance Herndon gushed as he stood behind an elaborate chocolate cake. His guests converged, champagne glasses in hand, as an air of drama swept the nightclub. The crowd split in two, opening an entryway for Gary Jenkins, the lead singer of Silk. He appeared in the aisle almost magically and began a suave stroll toward Lance, crooning as he approached.

Gary's tenor was strong and soul-drenched, soaring in a manner that cloaked the old familiar melody—"Happy birthday to you / Happy birthday to you"—in fanciful gospel timbre. Lance smiled broadly and flung his head back in that effeminate way that caused some to whisper from time to time that he was gay.

As was often the case at his gatherings, most of the guests to-night were women, many of whom could attest firsthand that Lance, at minimum, had derived much pleasure in them. One exception was Zonya Adams. Having worked for Lance for several years, Zonya admired her boss's business acumen, though she was repulsed by his womanizing and on several occasions told him so. Lance appreciated Zonya's wholesome manner and worked hard to keep his messy social affairs away from her.

Zonya had asked her husband, Gary, to come and serenade Lance tonight. She could never tell Lance this, but of late she had begun to feel sorry for him. It seemed to her that Lance had lost his way in life. Jeannine had left him, Access's billings had slowed considerably, and his foray into entertainment, an industry he had been trying to break into, had not been successful. Once he'd been an esteemed presence around town, but Lance's clout was mostly just an illusion now. Zonya knew as much. It was just a matter of time before others did, too.

With throngs of well-wishers gathered around him, Lance appeared to be at ease with his life. Yet to investigators who would later probe his death, the party not only offered a window into his confused private world but also offered crucial evidence about Lance's various states of affairs in the months leading up to his murder.

Lance was not much prone to self-reflection or pity, though he surely appreciated Gary's presence that night. Even without the birthday milestone, this party—hosted in the moonlit nightclub at the top of the Hilton—had attracted Atlanta's finest in women and music, his twin obsessions. Lance's love of women was something of an open secret around town, yet few were aware that toward the end of his life Lance had become fixated on breaking into the music business. To his confidants he often complained that he had become bored with the day-to-day salesmanship required to keep Access afloat, that he wanted to parlay his entrepreneurial talent into music. All day at work, his office television was now turned to BET. Favoring 1980s soul and funk and R & B, but lately having grown to appreciate rap, Lance would let the music videos play softly in the background as a kind of inspiration for a career change.

Indeed, when Lance had moved to Atlanta in the late 1970s, the world seemed tilted to favor his generation; whites had already begun their flight into the suburbs, leaving behind a cadre of young black professionals who, with Mayor Maynard Jackson at the helm, took their place as the entitled class. Yet over the past decade a rising tide of conservative, anti-affirmative-action policies in Georgia—and across the country, for that matter—had eroded this group's influence. Government contracts, more closely scrutinized than ever, were tougher for small black firms to win; corporations became less aggressive in their minority recruitment efforts; loans and grants for colleges had become harder to come by. In its heyday, Access had risen to become one of the nation's fastest-growing minority companies because there weren't many minority-owned companies with which to compete. Now the market was flooded with minority companies vying for a shrinking number of minority set-aside contracts. Many of these firms were simply better than Access.

Part of the problem, too, was that Lance wasn't keeping up with the technology in his field. Success in the industry required constant training and certification. Lance had majored in computer science back in the 1970s and never went back to school to freshen up. The result was that his knowledge was sorely outdated. As one of Lance's associates put it, "Lance had a great Rolodex, but he really didn't know shit about computers." There had been a point, in the early 1990s, when a rival firm had approached Lance with a generous offer to buy Access. Lance came to regret turning down that offer.

If Lance and his contemporaries had scored wearing navy blue suits and smart shoes and collecting business cards at power lunches, Atlanta's hot new players sported baggy jeans and diamond pinkie rings, drove souped-up SUVs, and flashed rolls of cash at the bar. While the children of black strivers were away at college, these rebels had quietly built an entertainment industry, an Atlanta-based modern Motown of record labels and artists and producers who were fast becoming wealthier than the city's black boomers had ever imagined. Of course, these local acts such as Ludacris, Outkast, and Lil Jon would also do their part in spawning a pop culture that celebrated black-on-black violence, defiled black women as "hoes," and adopted material gain as a moral compass.

Lance personally wasn't much for the bling style of the hip-hop generation, though he was staggered by the amount of cash that seemed to be flowing in their direction. He was far too proud to admit it, but he conceded to confidantes his fear that this younger crop of entrepreneurs portended his own extinction as a player. This partly explained Lance's fondness for Gary, whom Lance had watched morph from an unassuming churchgoing kid from Nashville into a music industry celebrity. Gary Jenkins, with his clean-shaven scalp and hip-hop swagger, embodied at least the aesthetic, though not the ghetto-glam mores, of many of the city's rising young stars.

Some four years ago, shortly after Zonya started working for Lance, her husband, Gary, had joined Silk, the all-male singing group formed by R & B star singer Keith Sweat. The group's 1992 debut album, *Lose Control,* included an ultra-sexual bedroom anthem called "Freak Me" that catapulted Silk into instant fame. Gary, who sang the tune's saucy hook, "Let me lick you up and down / Till you say stop" had deep reservations about recording the raunchy number when Keith Sweat suggested it: "I'm thinking,

What's my mama going to think? What are the people at the church going to think?"

Silk was performing in Amsterdam in 1993, and the fans' anticipation over the concert was feverish. "When we got to Amsterdam, we were going to do an in-store promotion," Gary says. "As we drove up, there was a big crowd waiting. We are getting out and they had to throw us back in the van, one by one, because this crowd was trying to get to us. They tore that little record store up, just ransacked it to the point where we couldn't even do the in-store. They started coming after the van, and we had to drive off. It was scary, like, 'Wow, we've really arrived like *that*? Is this real?' It was far more than I ever expected." Lance happened to be traveling in Amsterdam and spent some time hanging out with Gary, who shared what to him had been a frightening episode. Lance loved it. Later that night, Lance was at the concert bobbing like a teenager.

Upon his return to the States, Lance began a crusade to recast himself as a music mogul. The opportunity came when one of his former employees—a fellow who had worked part-time for Access while in college—approached him for a short-term loan, assuring him that he could repay it in a few months. When Lance inquired what the money was for, the fellow explained that he and his business partner were managing a new solo artist named Dionne Farris, an alternative soul singer who had most recently earned some acclaim as part of the Grammy-winning rap group Arrested Development. They had Farris in the studio recording an album, but a cash-flow crunch was slowing down the process. Lance wrote a check for eight thousand dollars, with two conditions attached: he took a few modern art pieces from the managers' office home with him as collateral, and a small percentage of the business.

While Farris's managers' plan was to repay Lance and break free of him, they failed to understand Lance's business style. As one of his associates recalled, "Lance made tons of loans, and they were all bad." In other words, Lance had no intentions of being repaid. What he wanted in exchange for his money was to be a part owner of an entertainment management company.

The managers' first sign that they had made a mistake came within a week after the deal was struck. An aspiring singer came into the management office asking for a meeting. When the receptionist asked who had sent her, she handed over a business card. It read: "Lance H. Herndon, principal, Pos Act Entertainment."

For eight thousand dollars, Lance had bought himself a new identity. But Lance's micromanaging style clashed with the loose, artsy music crowd that viewed him as an interloper, a wannabe. Worse, every time they looked up, there was Lance, requesting tickets for himself and his friends to Farris's performances in Los Angeles or New York, or dropping by and hanging around for hours during studio sessions, calling the office with unsolicited comments and critiques and analysis, and offering advice on the best direction for the music video. He even wanted to accompany the managers to Farris's meetings with Columbia Records executives. It was not uncommon for him to show up uninvited at exclusive industry parties, straight-faced, saying, "I'm Dionne Farris's manager, and I need to get in." He was driving Farris's camp nuts.

What made matters more awkward was that Herndon did not particularly like Farris's style of music. He liked popular, danceable music, not the bohemian, alternative brand of R & B Farris was recording. One night he stopped by one of Farris's recording sessions and found her in the vocal booth with a live snake slithering around her neck as she purred low and ethereal into the microphone. Lance thought she was tripping and wasting everyone's money. He went ballistic. "She needs to stop this foolishness and record some shake-your-booty music or something," he complained. The managers eventually refused to deal with Lance and requested that Zonya be made the intermediary until they could pay Lance back, which they did promptly before happily severing ties to him altogether.

The week before Lance died, during the Olympic Games festivities, Gary and Zonya spotted Lance and Kathi standing amid the crowd outside a sold-out Parliament Funkadelics concert at the House of Blues. Gary, who had been invited to the concert as a VIP, told Lance and Kathi to follow him as he cut through the crowd into an exclusive section and an awaiting table. At one point during the night, funk master George Clinton called Gary up on stage, where they grooved together to a blasting band. Lance was up on his feet, snapping a picture of the moment.

With both his venture in music management and the Vixen nightclub floundering, Lance increasingly sought refuge in women. At his birthday party that night, standing across the room, was Lacey Banks, her fair, shapely legs generously exposed by the slit in her black silk skirt. Lance took credit for inspiring Lacey to preen so, making her rethink the utility of her body parts. "Good girls might get what they want for Christmas, but bad girls get what they want all year long," Lance often told her. Earlier that evening, with a wink as her cue, she had followed him down to his hotel suite Jacuzzi, where she pleasured him—his girlfriend Kathi all the while mingling unaware about the party.

For more than a decade now, Lacey had remained Lance's favorite playmate. As he blew out his candles, Lacey stood at the outer fringe of the crowd, watching from afar. If there is power in proximity, Lacey had learned to amass hers in yards, keeping through the years a distance from Lance at special events such as this. She was secure enough in her place to give Lance's other women—for

some time, it had been his wife Jeannine, and lately it was Kathi—
the spotlight. If Lacey harbored any doubt that night about her im-
portance to Lance, it had been quickly dispelled in the bubbles of
the Jacuzzi.

It could be said that Lance Herndon, or perhaps the myth of
him, was borne by women whose goodwill he had won with gifts,
cash, and sexual adventure. Lance was not known to be romantic,
but he was, his male buddies agreed, masterful at pleasing a certain
type. His female companions tended to be educated, but not so
much, financially self-sufficient but needy nonetheless. In essence,
they wanted a man who could elevate their social status. Women
such as Lacey tended to wind up in Lance's orbit and avail them-
selves in abundance. As Ken Crooks had admitted about his friend,
Herndon could be quite a user of women. What he did not say was
that the terms were often quid pro quo. In Atlanta, where eligible
black women grossly outnumbered their male counterparts, Lance
had carte blanche to exploit the ratio.

There were, in fact, occasions when Lance paid Lacey for sexual
favors, but she did not view herself as anything less than a close
friend. She viewed Lance as a nurturer who helped restore the self-
esteem she had lost as a child. She trusted that Lance's interest in
her went far beyond sex. She never told Lance about the incident,
but when she was eight years old she was knocked off her bicycle
on a wooded path behind her home in Concord, North Carolina,
and raped. The passing years had helped her forget the details,
except that her assailant was a black man.

"I just remember the pain," she says quietly, eyes moist at the
memory. "It hurt so bad. I could barely stand up, but I was so
scared that I managed to drag myself home and lock myself in my
room. I was ashamed of what had happened to me. I didn't tell
anyone. I thought it was my fault. For years after, I felt ugly. I

stopped combing my hair, brushing my teeth, washing. I didn't want to be attractive. I grew out of that, but I have never got over what happened to me." Upon graduating high school, Lacey moved to Atlanta in the early 1980s and had found work as a bank teller at Wachovia when Lance stepped up to her window. "He told me I was pretty," she said. "Besides my parents, I had never been told that before."

Shortly after they began dating, Lance grew restless with conventional, one-on-one sex. He began challenging Lacey to fulfill various fantasies. He also proved to be increasingly generous to her, regularly depositing money into her checking account. She felt compelled, obligated even, to reciprocate. There was the time when, after he and she had made love one night, Lance ordered a pizza and challenged her to seduce the deliveryman when he arrived. She complied, and to this day she isn't quite sure whether Lance orchestrated the encounter or whether the pizza guy was an actual stranger. There were numerous such men, Lance's friends mostly, with whom she slept out of loyalty to Lance, sometimes one-on-one and on occasion as part of a ménage à trois. She also recruited women to join her and Lance in the bedroom. Of late, he had grown particularly fond of the chocolate-toned, bisexual woman that Lacey sometimes brought along. Satisfying Lance's robust sexual appetite became a kind of moonlighting job for Lacey, throughout his marriage to Jeannine and her own relationships with men.

Most recently, Lance had been dating Kathi, and he was candid with Lacey about this. Kathi was merely a trophy, he said, a public showpiece. She liked mingling among the affluent. Their relationship was built on little more than this fact, even if Kathi needed to believe otherwise. To make Kathi feel special, Lance kept a picture of her on his nightstand. Yet whenever Lacey was in his bedroom, she would turn the picture facedown, and they would laugh as they crawled into bed.

As Lance sliced into the big cake, his guests applauded and the deejay kicked back in with "Push It." Lance hugged Zonya and husband Gary, and the couple disappeared onto the crowded dance floor. Kathi was standing beside Lance, but he did not reach for her. Instead, he put his arm around a young woman, unfamiliar and standing nearby, and made her his dance partner. She was everything he liked: a petite size four, fair skin, dark straight hair. She was, in essence, a fresher, younger version of Kathi herself.

Anyone who has spent any time with Kathi Collins knows she has always fancied herself a diva of sorts; the quintessential Black American Princess, she possessed lavish tastes in food and fashion and was, in her own eyes, a source of positive karma for anyone wealthy enough to have her on his arm. Lance, who made a point of attending the Soul Train Awards each year, had met Kathi in Los Angeles in 1989 at a music industry party. Although both of them were married at the time, they began an affair. Their divorces—hers in 1995 and his from Jeannine in January 1996—cleared the way for her to relocate from the West Coast to Atlanta and explore the possibility of a deeper, more serious union. Lance had encouraged the move.

Most viewed Kathi as almost a caricature of class. Shortly after Jeannine divorced Lance, for instance, she made a formidable debut on the scene, tossing back her long hair and primping with such animation that Lance's staff could only roll its collective eyes and hope the affair proved the shortest of flings. Initially, they ignored her. Kathi was no fool, though, and sensing the staff's negative vibes, she opted not for a peace mission but rather a quiet counter-attack. The result: within weeks, Lance's staff grumbled as they picked up Kathi's dry cleaning and delivered it to his house, where she had amassed a considerable wardrobe in the master bedroom closet.

For the coveted role of Lance's number-one, Kathi Collins seemed to come straight out of central casting; she boasted a dark, wavy mane, high cheekbones, a finely bridged nose, and skin as fair as any Caucasian's. She also had a bombshell body—beneath her designer attire were curves generally sheathed in men's magazines. Lance pampered Kathi; within his stable of women, she was the one he took the most pride in showing off publicly. She was attractive, fashionable, and quick-witted, an ambitious woman herself, and he trusted her to understand by osmosis both his business and social agenda and to advance it when he wasn't around. He could take Kathi to the most exclusive black-tie event, and within an hour or so she would have harvested its most valuable contacts, handing Lance a small stack of business cards at the end of the night before sliding out of her Prada dress and running her bath. A graduate of the University of Seattle, she managed an upscale women's clothing boutique but was blessed with enough feminine gravitas to place her most anywhere she wanted.

But by his final birthday party, Kathi and Lance had begun to drift apart. She was getting to be too high-maintenance, and he was ready to move on. As Lance strolled around his soiree that night, champagne corks popped around him. Women gazed, touched his lapel, and smiled. One woman, sitting at a table with one of Lance's clients, caught his attention. This one had hazel eyes. Lance leaned over and introduced himself.

PART II

mistresses, motives, and murder

chapter seven

FOR THEY EXISTED

Great men leave this world differently than the rest of us. Their death prompts comparison, their deeds inspire awe, and when we ask ourselves in quiet bewilderment what the world would have looked like had they not lived, we know that somehow we are better off because they did. If dignitaries depart the earth drawn by horse and motorcade, the great ascend hauling the hope of an entire people on their backs. In the summer of 2003, Atlanta's first black mayor, Maynard Holbrook Jackson Jr., died of a heart attack at Reagan International Airport in Washington, D.C. He was sixty-five years old.

The influence of Maynard Jackson on Atlanta's black middle class had been nothing less than profound. Nearly every mid-career black professional in Atlanta finds themselves invariably referencing Maynard in pondering their own success. By extension, it is impossible to assess Lance Herndon's conquests independent of the political machine Maynard Jackson created solely to steer wealth into the hands of black entrepreneurs.

When Jackson took office in 1974, for instance, his first move was to call the good ole boys at the local banks, law firms, and construction companies and demand that they partner with, mentor, or just plain start hiring black folks or kiss their millions of dollars in local government contracts good-bye. A few told him to take a hike, but most grumbled and did as they were told. While less than 1 percent of the city's contracts were awarded to minorities when he took office, over the next five years that number had risen to nearly 40 percent, and a few years later some 80 percent of all contracts awarded at U.S. airports were in Atlanta. By making sure that black contractors got a piece of the expansion of the airport, Jackson boasted that he had created twenty-five new black millionaires. The spirit of such pro-black bravado traveled fast, prompting thousands of blacks to head south to Atlanta. One of them was Lance Herndon.

Upon hearing news of Jackson's death, black Atlanta seemed to stop cold in its tracks, as if the gilded boulevards on which it had been cruising might turn back to dirt roads. The grief was rooted in symbolism; Jackson had retired from public office back in 1994 and had since devoted much of his energy to brokering municipal deals through an investment banking firm whose shingle bore his name. Still, in the private sector Jackson continued to enjoy a kind of mythic adulation among black Atlantans—a devotion evident over two days in the masses who lined up in pounding heat in front of City Hall to view the man's body as it lay in state, in the crowds who skipped work to file past his body at the Martin Luther King Chapel at Morehouse College, his alma mater.

His passing was fused into an already emotional time throughout the South. During the same week he died, there was news that two prominent segregationists, U.S. Senator Strom Thurmond of South Carolina and Lester Maddox, the former Georgia governor, had passed away. The three deaths brimmed with irony. Strom Thurmond was known for his 1948 campaign for president on the "Dixiecrat" platform of segregation, while Lester Maddox had earned his way into the hearts of southern bigots in the early 1960s by brandishing a pistol and chasing some black diners in Atlanta out of his Pickrick Restaurant.

A formidable presence, Jackson stood a barrel-chested six foot three inches, spoke in a king's melodic baritone, and possessed a soft touch with the urban poor that belied his aristocratic pedigree. Jackson could flout the imprimatur of white power brokers because he himself was already part of a privileged class. Born in Houston and raised in a deeply segregated Atlanta, he grew up a member of the black southern elite, the arc of his bloodline tracing a path back to his maternal grandfather, John Wesley Dobbs, son of Georgia slaves whose influence in the Atlanta black business community in the 1930s earned him the moniker "the Mayor of Sweet Auburn." Among his many achievements, Dobbs founded the Negro Voters League and reigned as grand master of the Prince Hall Masons. Jackson's father, the Reverend Maynard Jackson Sr., was no slouch either as pastor of Atlanta Friendship Baptist Church, a bedrock institution of the city's black middle class. Maynard Jackson's mother was a Spelman College professor who earned a doctorate in French from the University of Toulouse. She spoke French so often at home that young Maynard was fluent by fourteen, the young age at which he enrolled in Morehouse College as a freshman.

Jackson came of age when Atlanta remained deeply segregated; when City Hall had a separate cafeteria, drinking fountains, and restrooms for blacks; when black police officers dressed in the basement of the black YMCA on Butler Street and were prohibited from arresting whites; when blacks made up a third of the city's population, yet there were no black elected officials. It was a city where, when Dr. Martin Luther King Jr. was awarded a Nobel Peace Prize in 1964, the city's white business leaders scoffed at the notion of a dinner in his honor, attending only grudgingly after Coke chairman Robert Woodruff threatened to move the company. "We can't operate from a base where our town is reviled," he warned. "Coke doesn't need Atlanta. It's up to you whether Atlanta needs Coke."

Jackson ultimately came to believe that black Atlanta needed him. "I remember going out one night with Julian Bond and his first wife, Alice," recalls the late mayor's first wife, Bunnie Jackson-Ransom. "This was years ago—Maynard and I had just gotten married, and we were living in an apartment. Julian was driving, and we were out looking for a Chinese restaurant that would serve us. We couldn't find a Chinese restaurant in all of Atlanta that would serve us. And I remember Julian and Maynard were sitting up front talking politics, and Julian said, 'I think I'm going to make a run for the House.' And Maynard said, 'Are you sure you know what you're doing?' And Julian said, 'Yeah, I got a few people—he was talking about SNCC—who are going to go door-to-door and ring some bells, and I think we can pull it off.' I remember that conversation like it was yesterday. Julian was talking about running for the

House of Representatives, and Maynard hadn't even thought about running for mayor. His goal was to have his own law firm.

"And then not long after, Kennedy was assassinated. And then King was assassinated. I was away in North Carolina visiting my family, and by the time I got back Maynard had quit his job. Maynard is a very emotional guy, a very I'm-going-to-save-the-world person. He had been working at the Emory University law clinic. We had just bought a house, and we had a six-week-old baby. But he decided to get involved in politics. He borrowed three thousand dollars to run against Herman Talmadge in Georgia. It scared me. I thought somebody was going to shoot him. If they didn't shoot him, I *certainly* was going to, because he had quit his job and we had no money. Maynard went around in an airplane that some pilot had—a black guy—and he started campaigning. And he carried the Atlanta vote. That's when the political bug bit him."

Upon winning the mayor's office in 1974, Jackson vowed an administration that would "afford even the poorest and most destitute person an alternative to agony." If the vision earned him affection among the black masses, it raised the ire of a white establishment that lambasted his championing of affirmative action as "racial quotas." Jackson took on his foes with fury. "There are some who are not my friends who resent the fact that I work hard to get blacks into a position of equal opportunity," he once told a group of reporters. "My response is: To hell with them."

Jackson relished his bully pulpit. Once, when the Atlanta Falcons were playing in their home stadium, Jackson had sent over greetings from his fair city that he wanted commentators Howard Cosell and Frank Gifford to read during their *Monday Night Football* telecast. When the request was rejected, Jackson couriered over a less friendly message, giving them two options. The first was to read his greeting. The other was to play the second half in the dark, because he was going to order that the stadium lights be shut off. Jackson, of course, got his way. There was the time, too, when Jackson, preparing to speak one early Saturday morning on the Morehouse College campus, was met by student complaints over the city's poor garbage collection in the area. Jackson stepped away from the microphone, disappeared inside one of the buildings, and returned to continue speaking. Minutes later, as he was making his final remarks, several garbage trucks came rolling onto campus. He ended his speech to a chorus of students roaring with delight.

At Jackson's funeral, former president Bill Clinton stood behind the podium and enthused about how the late mayor's "creamy voice could melt the meanness out of the hardest heart." Coretta Scott King, first lady of Atlanta and the widow of civil rights leader and Nobel Peace Prize recipient Dr. Martin Luther King Jr., told the crowd that Jackson was an "incorruptible champion of the poor and oppressed, the disadvantaged and the downtrodden," while the Reverend Joseph Lowry of the civil rights organization the Southern Christian Leadership Council opined that "Maynard Jackson set the standard for the public servant who is bold enough to challenge the establishment and bad enough to stand the storm that ensued." The famous Georgia congressman John Lewis somberly pronounced his old friend "one of the founding fathers of the New Atlanta, the New South and the New America."

Indeed, many of the old-timers at the funeral could remember as though yesterday a humbler time when blacks had no voice, no economic clout, but only a belief that we were all as poor as the poorest among us. They could recall a voting rally as far back as sixty years before, in 1935, in the heart of the city on Auburn Avenue, or what was known back then as "The Negro Peachtree." They had marched for their rights that day, side by side in two orderly rows along Auburn, the men dressed neatly in dark suits and ties, the women in knee-length dresses. Over the previous fifty years, blacks had risen fiercely from servitude, earning degrees in science and literature and history from the city's five black colleges, as well as opening grocery stores and pharmacies and insurance companies and other businesses catering to Atlanta's growing black middle class. And they had believed in glorifying more than themselves, but their whole race. They came together that day and formed a dark ribbon beneath cloudy gray skies, moving along in quiet dignity, passing by Ebenezer Baptist Church on the corner of Jackson and Auburn Avenue en route to City Hall. Leading the march was Martin Luther King Sr., a tall commanding figure sporting a suit and white-banded fedora, who at one point in the procession stopped in his tracks and called out to the crowd, passion thundering in his voice. "I know one thing," he declared to the crowd, "I ain't gonna plow no more mules. I'll never step off the road again to let white folks pass. I am going to move toward freedom, and I'm hoping everybody with me here today is going to go right along with me."

At Jackson's funeral, Vernon Jordan, the Atlanta native and distinguished civil rights attorney, appeared onstage and tried to sum up his friend's life. "Maynard Jackson lived because he shared the action and passion of his times," Jordan said. "But beyond that, Maynard Jackson was on the *right* side of history."

chapter eight

THE PROSECUTOR

On a crisp January morning in 1997, Assistant District Attorney Clint Rucker strolled into Salaam's, the popular barbershop on Atlanta's east side, and tossed the question of Lance Herndon's death into air already charged with buzzing clippers, raucous chatter, and the ever-present thump of soul music. Actually, as he and other barbershop patrons who were present that day would later recall, Clint didn't pose the question immediately. First he scanned the joint to make sure none of his enemies were around, any ex-cons or relatives of folks he'd had locked up who might be eager to seek vengeance on neutral ground. Satisfied he was among only the usual Saturday regulars, who nodded and grunted their greetings, Rucker settled his beefy frame into one of the vinyl seats jumbled along the wall and spoke in the commanding baritone that always made folks sit up and listen.

"All right, fellas," he called out. "I gotta question for y'all. Remember the millionaire brother out in Roswell, the one they found dead with his head all bashed in a few months back?"

That Lance Herndon had become fodder for conversation at Salaam's brims with paradox, considering his affinity for high-end suburban salons. He kept a regular appointment with a beloved male hairstylist known simply as Van, whose prodigious talents and battery of chemicals were never quite enough to bring Lance's coarse, woolly head into the soft submission Lance desired. In Clint Rucker's world, however, aside from giving a good haircut, few places were more useful than Salaam's, a tidy little barbershop tucked away in a forlorn strip mall, flanked by a rib shack and a storefront church. Salaam's was the true "high court," where the verdict was always swift and unforgiving. Whenever Clint wanted a frank assessment of how one of his cases might play before a jury, he could usually hand it to the crowd at Salaam's, let them kick it around for a while, and walk away with a semi-reliable analysis of the case's hot buttons and soft spots.

Founded some forty years ago by Clarence Salaam, a mild-mannered Muslim fellow, Salaam's was a neighborhood institution of sorts. Unlike most other barbershops in the area, where the atmosphere was often boisterous and unruly, Salaam's worked to maintain the air of dignified, respectful, high-mindedness that founder Clarence valued and demanded of patrons. Instead of the usual shop fare of leggy pinup girls, malt liquor ads, and faded cabaret flyers on the walls, the decor at Salaam's was decidedly uplifting rather than a reflection of its hard-core habitat. In a community rife with drug addiction, teenage pregnancy, and gun violence, Salaam's strived to be an oasis from such pathology, its walls adorned with pastel images of black families playing and praying together. The only worldly intrusion, save its patrons, emanated from the large-screen television mounted to the ceiling and the radio tuned to play anything but gangsta rap stations.

There were moments, of course, when Salaam's genteel atmosphere was overwhelmed by the sheer force of the streets surrounding it, by the bluster and passion of men unable to check their crude alleyway lingo and streetwise ideology for Allah, or anyone else for that matter. There were moments when one of the proprietors would start a well-intentioned dialogue about sports, weather, or politics—or even the federal deficit—and the arc of the discussion would inevitably drift from inspired debate to a peak in interest, followed by yawns and boredom, and finally an artful segue back to the favorite subjects of women and sex, with such remarks as, "So long as the U.S. gub'ment ain't runnin' a pussy deficit—me, personally, I really don't give a shit," upon which Clarence would glare at the patron and wave a disapproving finger. "Not in here, my man. Uh-uh, you gotta take that language outside."

While old Clarence still reigned as a kind of etiquette policeman, his role in the shop had diminished; a few years ago he had sold his interest to his young apprentice, Joe, a stout fellow around thirty-five whose hip-hop demeanor belied a quietly rigid work ethic. On this particular day, Joe was focused on the tedious task of carving an intricate design into the back of a teenage customer's hair, pausing briefly as Clint continued posing his question to customers awaiting it in rapt silence: "I wanna know whether y'all think a woman of average size, about five-foot-three, a hundred-ten pounds, could beat a man to death?"

The question triggered lots of joking and guffawing and quipping before things turned quiet again. Cupcake, brightly dressed and Jheri-curled, slid his cell phone into his shirt pocket, his dark face attentive. Clint could see that his question had all of Salaam's customers thinking, as old Hubert, a retired mechanic who was nearly deaf, mumbled "Five-foot-three, huh?" And for the first time in Clint's recent memory, even sullen old Smitty, a recovering alcoholic and former history professor at Clark College, raised his beady eyes above the pages of his *Atlanta Journal-Constitution* and asked whether Clint happened to be working on the Lance Herndon case. Adhering to barbershop etiquette, which rules out coyness, Clint allowed that officially he had not yet been given the case, but that this one was likely to wind up on his desk.

So, Smitty had been wondering, was this fellow related to the late Alonzo Herndon? Clint Rucker told him, not to his knowledge, he wasn't. But by then Smitty had already shifted his eyes back to his newspaper, apparently less interested in the tragedy of a high-rolling newcomer than a blood relative to the patriarch of Atlanta's first truly rich black family. Indeed, few names in Atlanta divide its black nouveau riche and its old established money more sharply than that of the late Alonzo Herndon, the son of a slave mother and her white master who rose to become the most successful black businessman in the city's history.

Black Atlantans learn the story of Alonzo Herndon as early as kindergarten; about how he was born in the small farming community of Social Circle, Georgia, forty miles east of Atlanta, and at twenty years old fled the plantation in which he grew up for Jonesboro, where he trained as a barber. With his soft wavy hair and olive skin, Herndon himself looked like a white man, though he proudly embraced his blackness. He also proved to be a shrewd entrepreneur, and by the late 1800s he had moved to Atlanta and built a successful chain of upscale barbershops that attracted droves of white affluent customers. His showpiece was a twenty-five-chair emporium at 66 Peachtree Street, a shop so opulent it was dubbed the

Crystal Palace. With his barbershop empire flourishing, Herndon forayed into real estate, as well as founding the Atlanta Life Insurance Company, which remains one of the largest black-owned insurance companies in the nation. Herndon died in 1927, but his legacy is still memorialized everywhere, from Atlanta Life's mammoth headquarters bordering downtown to the family's classical-style mansion, a popular tourist destination with a magnificent backyard view of the entire Atlanta skyline.

Old Smitty eventually looked up from his newspaper and grunted something to Clint about it standing to reason that anyone could kill anyone under the right emotional circumstance. Weight, gender—those things didn't matter much. Cupcake disagreed, belly laughing: "no itty-bitty babe" could beat a regular-sized man to death unless he was asleep or tied up.

"You got that right," Joe chimed in, recalling how "this one chick," a large-sized woman, tried to swing on him. "I had her in a headlock so fast it wasn't funny." He'd been upset enough to fight her back, but he didn't. Instead, he held her until she calmed down. No matter how big she was, it just wouldn't have been a fair fight. "A woman just can't beat up a dude, unless maybe he's a sissy," he said.

"Okay, okay," Rucker cut in. "What if she was in a rage? Say the dude cheated on her or was a big spender who bought her everything she wanted but was cutting her off? How about then?"

Clint's revised scenario still did not impress his audience. In fact, Cupcake declared, albeit in his own street vernacular, that such a femme fatale theory now seemed far less plausible because it involved putting her own financial livelihood at stake. The average gold-digging woman enjoyed her material possessions too much to permanently put her most generous benefactor out of business, a hideously counterproductive act without the promise of a huge insurance windfall. The more likely recourse in the situation Clint had outlined was for the woman to try and win him back by making him reassess her value as a companion, probably by offering him more or better sex, which was always a potent weapon against a waffling sugar daddy. Most all women understand their male counterparts to be pathetically weak against sex, and will mostly seek to control them through tenderness rather than force, he explained.

That morning, the conversation ended on a sour note, with Joe telling Clint what a shame it was that this brother Lance Herndon had bootstrapped his way to being a millionaire, was in the prime of his life, and somebody came and murdered him in cold blood—and the only person being targeted as a suspect was a sister he was sleeping with. Gold-digger or not, something didn't quite sound right. Clint tried to explain that Lance Herndon was a real player, the kind of brother who rarely went to bed alone. Still, there was a collective disbelief around the barbershop that a woman murdered him. Joe, having heard enough and spoken his mind, went back to cutting his customer's hair, but not without first reminding Clint about those lazy racist cops in Los Angeles who prematurely singled out O. J. Simpson. Those cops in Roswell need to keep looking, he said, because a rich man like Lance Herndon surely had plenty of enemies, the least likely of which were women.

It is around nine o'clock on a Saturday night and the corridors of the Fulton County Courthouse are dead quiet. Sitting in his office, Clint Rucker pauses and looks over at the cardboard boxes stacked up beside his desk. Inside the boxes are reams of documents from the Lance Herndon murder investigation and trial. Clint reaches over and thumps the cardboard with one of his big fingers, as though Lance himself was trapped inside.

STATE'S
EXHIBIT
4

Lance Harrison Herndon, a native of New York City, was among the thousands of ambitious blacks who migrated to Atlanta during the 1970s and 1980s. He founded Access, Inc., an information systems consulting firm that was cited for excellence by presidents George H. W. Bush and Bill Clinton. (*Courtesy of Fulton County District Attorneys Office*)

FROM JANUARY UNTIL DECEMBER
EVERYONE HAS A DAY THAT THEY
HAVE TO REMEMBER
MAYBE TURNING 21 OR 95
IT'S
LANCE H. HERNDON'S
BIRTHDAY
COME ON GET ___ !!!

FRIDAY, APRIL 12, 1996
10:00 P.M. UNTIL 2:00 A.M.
ANOTHER WORLD
ROOF TOP OF THE ATLANTA HILTON
255 COURTLAND STREET

ATTIRE: YOUR STYLE

ABSOLUTELY NO ADMISSION WITHOUT INVITATION
ADMITS TWO

STATE'S
EXHIBIT
32

Lance was popular on Atlanta's social scene. In the spring of 1996, he invited a couple hundred friends and colleagues to celebrate his forty-first birthday at a high-rise nightclub downtown. (Courtesy of Fulton County District Attorney's Office)

Lance and his bride, Jeannine Price, built their 6,000-square-foot dream home in Northcliff, a gated subdivision in Roswell. Their marriage split soon after, and Jeannine became an early suspect in her ex-husband's death. (*Courtesy of Fulton County District Attorneys Office*)

Access, Inc., was located in Lance's home in a spacious downstairs office suite. Suspicions arose when Lance, known for his obsession for punctuality and routine, failed to appear at work one morning. (*Courtesy of Fulton County District Attorneys Office*)

Lance's nude and severely bludgeoned corpse puzzled investigators. The crime scene had a strong sexual element, from a porn tape in a videocassette recorder, to an unopened pack of condoms, to Lance's naked body. Oddly, the three alarm clocks in the room were unplugged, as was the telephone beside his bed. (*Courtesy of Fulton County District Attorneys Office*)

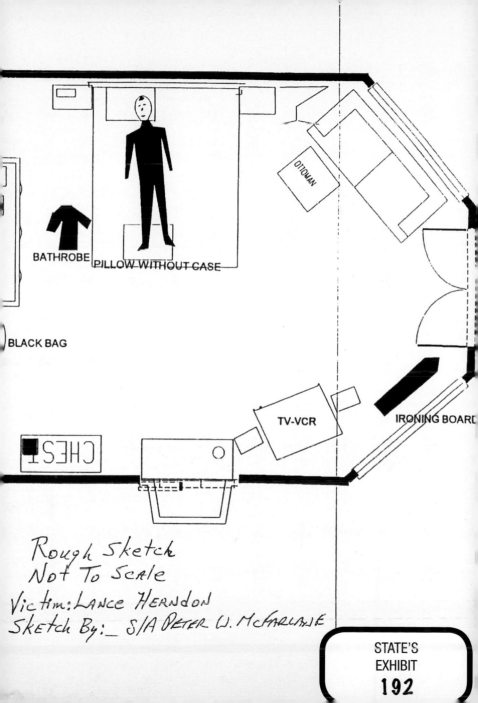

OTTOMAN

BATHROBE

PILLOW WITHOUT CASE

BLACK BAG

TV-VCR

IRONING BOARD

CHEST

Rough Sketch
Not To Scale
Victim: Lance Herndon
Sketch By: S/A Peter W. McFarlane

Blood spatter on the bedroom walls and headboard suggested that Lance's killer was straddling his chest when delivering the blows. Investigators determined that the V-shaped, dark-to-light pattern of the spatter was indicative of a clubbing motion. (*Courtesy of Fulton County District Attorneys Office*)

Police surmised that after bludgeoning Lance to death, his assailant wiped off the blood from their own body with this pillowcase that was discovered soaking in a commode in the bedroom suite bathroom. (*Courtesy of Fulton County District Attorneys Office*)

Kathi Collins appreciated Lance's high-style of living, and she began dating him seriously after his divorce from Jeannine. Police discovered this picture of Kathi turned face-down on Lance's nightstand while studying the crime scene. *(Courtesy of Fulton County District Attorneys Office)*

Lacey Banks, the last person to see Lance alive, became a primary suspect in his murder. As Lance's longtime mistress, Lacey was among the several women to whom Lance had provided credit cards. *(Courtesy of Lacey Banks)*

Like Lance, Clint is innately gifted and driven in his profession. He doesn't have to—or rather need to—fuss with the myopia or abstractions of his work; he simply looks at the problem, gets a vision of how to fix it, and just goes out and does it. The work is more instinctive than intellectual to him. He is good at prying, discussing, resolving. This talent, coupled with a sense of earnestness that melts juries, has led to his winning some very big cases.

At thirty-seven, Clint Rucker had become the envy of nearly every prosecutor in the DA's office. A protégé of District Attorney Paul Howard, the first black in Georgia elected to that office, Clint can hardly walk the streets without folks recognizing him from some high-profile case he prosecuted. "I try not to pay attention to all that stuff," Clint says. "One day you can be flyin' high, and the next day somebody's trying to tear you down."

Clint's voice is a floating folksy baritone that is music all its own. "Let me tell you somethin'," he goes on. "When I was young, all I wanted to do was shoot hoops. And I was getting into all kinds of trouble in school, too. Every day, somethin' else. Teachers calling home. Fights. Just actin' a *fool.* That's part of the reason my mom moved us out of Harlem."

It is easy to imagine Big Clint busting heads in Harlem. The man stands six-foot-two, weighs about two hundred forty pounds, all packed tight in one grandly muscular frame. Clint had been a star quarterback at Druid Hills High School, able, when necessary, to brutishly trample his way into the end zone with opponents hanging onto his jersey. Upon graduating from Emory University, Clint went on to study law at Thurgood Marshall Law School at Texas Southern University.

At the courthouse, some colleagues are quick to dismiss Clint as overrated. They grumble that his work ethic is suspect, saying that he is frequently ill prepared for trial, that he places less value in substance than style. Clint shrugs off such criticism. While his organizational skills could admittedly be better, he says, his work-load is often more demanding than that of most of the other assistant DAs. His cases tend to be bigger, and more complex. As for the style-over-substance thing, he refers to his record: he has won convictions in virtually every case he has tried. He suspects the reason is because he understands what many of his colleagues do not, which is that serving up the law cold to juries is not effective. Juries tend to be swayed less by hard fact and direct evidence than a solid, reasonable, and well-articulated scenario that led to some law being broken. Clint takes prides in being better than most at spinning a believable yarn.

Clint's appeal to juries is also largely physical. He dresses with noticeable cosmopolitan flair; the colorful hand-woven silk tie, the sparkle of silver cuff links at his wrists, the expensive black leather lace-ups crowned by the cuff of elegantly draped slacks. But it is his sheer body mass that astounds, the portion of the room he fills. His Italian business suits scarcely camouflage his lumberjack frame; his neck juts with tree-stump girth from his collar, his burly arms making the bailiff's look twiggy by comparison.

Yet the Titan physique is softened by his big jovial face, the lively eyes and toothy grin that blend into the countenance of a gentle giant. In the courtroom, Rucker's affable mug atop such a mighty frame is disarming to jurors. The authority he achieves through his physical size, and that is cemented in his role as a prosecutor, Clint gives back to jurors with generous portions of pure congeniality and country boy manners, yes ma'am and no sir and thankyamuch and all the polite touches that endear a man his size to a world conditioned to root for a brute whose mama taught him well.

chapter nine

EVIDENCE OF
THINGS NOT SEEN

As Clint had anticipated, five months after Lance Herndon's murder, two officials from the Roswell Police Department headed into downtown Atlanta to present evidence against the woman believed to have killed Lance Herndon, and to gauge the Fulton County District Attorney's willingness to seek a grand jury indictment against her. As the elevator rose to the sixth floor of the County Courthouse, the men—Detective Anastasio and his boss, Roswell police chief Edwin Williams, strode quietly through the corridor toward District Attorney Paul Howard's office. Anastasio was clutching against his hip a set of thick three-ring binders containing the details of his investigation into the homicide.

Howard greeted them warmly and told them how eager he was

to move this case forward. He also introduced them to Clint Rucker, whom he introduced as his very talented assistant DA in the newly formed Special Cases Division.

"You'll like working with Clint," he assured them. "He's one of our best."

Chief Williams opened the meeting by explaining that his department's investigation of the case had been anything but a cakewalk, that his guys had worked hard but still hadn't gotten all the goods they'd like to have. What they had was largely circumstantial, he said, but frankly, he wasn't sure there was much more to be reasonably obtained. There weren't any eyewitnesses to turn to, just folks in the house when the body was discovered. And there wasn't a trace of physical evidence connecting any of those women to his death.

Paul Howard asked what solid evidence they did have. Anastasio dropped the set of binders on the desk. Howard sat silently in his chair, leafing through the pages. After a few moments he looked up.

"Gentleman," he said finally, "please tell me this isn't all we've got."

Unfortunately for Anastasio, it was. Physical evidence from the crime scene had proven to be dreadfully scarce: investigators had searched Dumpsters, combed portions of the Chattahoochee and wooded lots in the surrounding area, and still hadn't found a murder weapon. His men had photographed a couple of footprint impressions from the carpet, honeycomb in pattern, and those appeared, at least based on their large size, to be a male's. But there also was no sign of forced entry into the home, which led them to believe that Lance's killer was someone he knew or had invited in. The three unplugged alarm clocks in the room, as well as the unplugged telephone, seemed to fit that theory.

And then, of course, they had Lance Herndon's naked and blud-geoned body, which showed no defensive wounds whatsoever, along with those godawful bloody sheets and pillowcases. What-ever occurred that night, the scene spelled sex: the pack of unused condoms, two pornographic videotapes, one in the television VCR and another on the nightstand. Anastasio had sent the pubic and head hairs discovered in Lance Herndon's bed to the lab for analy-sis. So far, the hair told him nothing except that Lance got laid a lot. There were enough random strands of head and pubic hair on this guy's sheets to rival a sorority-house bath. For hair samples even to be considered as usable evidence, Anastasio would need to narrow down the time of death enough to place someone specific inside that time frame—someone whose hair matched those found in the bed. Based on witness interviews, the only thing Anastasio could say with any certainty was that Lance Herndon was killed some-time between 8:00 P.M., the time Herndon left his mother's apart-ment after the family dinner, and around 10:20 A.M. the following morning, when his mother called 911. Phone records showed a phone call to Lacey around eleven that night, but nobody had actu-ally seen him make the call.

Further complicating the question of Lance Herndon's time of death was the fact that Herndon died on his waterbed. Because of this, Dr. Sperry, the medical examiner, had been extra cautious in even venturing a guess about the time of demise, explaining to An-astasio that it is not possible to accurately or reliably determine a time of death, no matter what the movies say. He talked about how some in his field had devoted their entire careers to finding a magic test or combination of things that would allow the profession to de-termine how long somebody has been dead, and each time, the theory came up short.

Sperry had then gone on to offer what sounded to Anastasio

more like a riddle than a probable time of death. The one thing Sperry knew for sure, he said, was that the victim was on a water-bed, and that the temperature of the waterbed was 88 degrees. The victim's body temperature at the time an investigator first examined it was 87 degrees, which basically meant that his body could have cooled down from a normal human body temperature of 98.6 to the temperature of the waterbed. He also knew that in death the human body loses about one to one and a half degrees of heat per hour, approximately. The downside of assessing this homicide, of course, was that even if the victim had lain there for another day or so, his temperature would have still been about 87 or 88 degrees because the waterbed would keep his temperature constant.

The other troubling factor was that the victim was covered with a blanket, which would also insulate the body. Sperry would have to speculate a time frame moving back in hours. The degree of stiffening of his body and other factors were certainly compatible with a time on the order of six to eight hours, though it could be a bit longer. Still, Sperry's best estimate based upon the physical findings was that the victim had been dead six to eight hours, maybe longer, before the time the body was first examined, which was about 11:00 A.M. This would make the time of death between 3:00 and 5:00 A.M. At the earliest, the death could have occurred at around 11:00 P.M. the previous night. Of course, Sperry added, looking at other factors like phone calls and when Herndon was last seen would be even more helpful in narrowing the time of death.

Detective Anastasio had found himself swimming in theories, leads, and advice from various tipsters—most of which steered him, always with great confidence, into what turned out to be dead ends. The dearth of evidence, both physical and circumstantial, meant he had little choice but to listen to even the most outlandishly spun tales. One tipster's suspicions that a gay street hustler had killed

Herndon had briefly gotten Anastasio's attention, at least until the woman added matter-of-factly that she did not know Herndon and had never even heard of the man until reading about his death in the newspaper. Her strong beliefs about the case, she said, arose from her gift of clairvoyance.

Another caller—she identified herself as Rhonda Gillis—spoke also of her suspicion that Herndon was gay. She, though, was an actual acquaintance of Herndon's. Miss Gillis reported having seen Herndon the previous Saturday night at Africa House, an old Presbyterian church on Courtland Street that had been leased for the Olympic gatherings. She recalled walking over to greet Lance, who was standing very close to another man. It was "obvious" to her that the men came to the party as a couple, she said. Herndon's friend was definitely gay, and was "completely oblivious" to her, barely engaging in her brief conversation with Lance. Lance spent all night talking to the man, not socializing with any of the women there. Gillis emphasized that it was entirely possible that Lance was bisexual because Atlanta was full of bisexual black men who were in the closet, men on the so-called down-low, as many called themselves.

Indeed, among the criticisms of Anastasio's investigation was his soft-pedaling of suspicions that Lance was bisexual. At the crime scene, GBI forensics expert Sam House had suggested that the murder had the classic elements of a homosexual tryst gone awry. The porn tapes—which in fact featured heterosexual sex—and condoms and the victim's nude state strongly hinted at a sexual encounter. But it was the powerful blows to the victim's face that House said were typically masculine responses to rage. Unless Anastasio could turn up a witness or a murder weapon that connected Herndon's body to a suspect and possible motive, House insisted, the homosexual angle should be among Anastasio's first pursuits.

In fairness, Detective Anastasio did pose the question of Lance's sexuality to his ex-wife, Jeannine. He asked her whether at any time, to her knowledge, Mr. Herndon had ever been involved in a homosexual or bisexual relationship. She said she was aware that some people questioned Lance's sexuality. A couple of years ago, for example, one of her girlfriends had asked her whether Lance was bisexual, and not even a year ago another friend had asked her the same question. But Jeannine personally had always disregarded such suspicions.

Jeannine admitted that her ex-husband was in ways quite vain. He was almost obsessively fastidious about his hygiene—he showered as many as three or four times on most days, kept a regular appointment at the salon for weekly manicures and pedicures, and was so concerned about keeping his nail beds clean that he would only eat barbecued ribs with a knife and fork. Admittedly, she wasn't aware of many heterosexual men who did that. But that's just how he was, and some people may have read too much into it. There was nothing in their marriage, though, that made her suspect that Lance was anything but heterosexual.

One of the strongest leads that came to Anastasio, in fact, centered on a woman. The tip came from Herndon's neighbor, a white corporate lawyer who a couple of weeks after the murder told investigators that on the morning of August 8, at approximately 4:45 A.M., he was driving out of the subdivision when he saw a small compact car, silver or champagne in color, sitting around the corner from his residence, its interior dome light on. Initially, Hodge figured the vehicle's occupant was a newspaper delivery person, but as he turned from Bluffview Trace onto Northcliff Trace, he said, he glimpsed the driver. She was a black female, not dark like Lance but fair-skinned. And her hair was pulled back. Upon seeing Hodge, she pulled off and drove out of the subdivision.

———

Lance had several telephone lines in his home and in his office, as well as two cellular phones and a pager. On August 7 and 8 there were hundreds of incoming and outgoing calls on each. Anastastio, along with his team of investigators, spent several hours tracking each of them back to the caller. Among them was Brandy West, who had phoned Lance a few hours before his probable time of death, sometime between midnight and 4:00 A.M., and then again a few hours after his body was discovered. In both instances she left a voice message, the first stating that she would be mailing some money out to him that day, and a final time to express concern that he had not yet phoned her back. Both calls were traced back to her home in San Francisco.

Brandy West made it clear that she and Lance had been close friends for many years, starting when she was a student at Emory University. They regularly talked long distance and were intimate when she was there or he came out on business. They saw each other pretty heavily in the mid-1980s, and never lost touch. Brandy is a married woman now, a computer specialist in San Francisco, but she explained that Lance had loaned her a few thousand dollars just a few months before, and that she was repaying him in monthly installments. Her calls to him that morning were simply to notify Lance of her timely payment. She also expressed surprise that the house alarm wasn't on the night he was killed. Lance was obsessed over his security system, she said, and kept it on all the time. The only other person who knew the code besides him was his ex-wife Jeannine.

In a discussion, Brandy reflected on her relationship with Lance, recalling that it actually began with a gift, a box of Godiva chocolates, which had arrived on her desk at the bank where she worked back in the spring of 1985. As with the other gifts that followed—a bouquet of freshly cut roses, bottles of vintage wine, concert tickets, cute Hallmarks—Lance had sent the candy anonymously. If Brandy was initially alarmed by the gift, figuring her phantom admirer was probably some lonely weirdo with too much time and money at his disposal, she relished the attention. A secretary, twenty-one years old, working to put herself through school at Emory University, Brandy figured she ought to treat herself to some of life's spoils while still young and pretty enough to enjoy them.

Brandy has smooth walnut skin and the silky shoulder-length hair and toned physique of the health-club enthusiast she has always been. Considering Herndon's preference for lighter-skinned women, she was surprised by his interest in her. She attributes the compromise to her wavy hair and smooth "island" complexion.

She recalls her first meeting with Lance on a sunny April afternoon. Brandy had left work early, and she was standing alone at the bus stop on Piedmont Street, wearing a yellow sundress. Her petite curves slowed traffic. When a burgundy BMW cruised up along the curb, Brandy feigned aloofness—until its dapper driver spoke her name, his crisp enunciation matched by an equally crisp French-cuffed shirtsleeve coolly perched in the open car window.

"I know you, Brandy," the man said. "You work for a client of mine, John Smiley over at First Atlanta. Where you headed?"

She eyed him closely. She vaguely recalled the stranger's face. "To a doctor's appointment," she said. "Out in Decatur."

"C'mon, let me give you a lift."

It was Lance's worldly air that initially attracted her to him; physically, Lance was not at all her type. Having grown up in a small rural town in northeast Georgia, she preferred big rugged guys, brash brothers with a hint of daring. Lance, in both his soft speaking voice and delicate manner, had something of a feminine aura—enough to give her pause. As he confessed to sending the gifts, Brandy, only half listening, studied his small manicured fingers perched on the steering wheel, the fine gray gabardine suit jacket hanging neatly on the back of the passenger-side seat. Yet as she inhaled the interior's leathery scent—the aroma mingled with the subtle musk of the driver's cologne—she found herself sitting beside him, the car lurching into gear, and Piedmont rushing by her window.

"So your appointment is way out in Decatur, huh. Well, rather than my driving you, I've got a better idea."

Before she could respond, Lance had swung an impressive U-turn and was headed back west on Piedmont. He picked up his car phone, dialed, and was looking directly into Brandy's eyes when he spoke. "Hey, Hal. We ready over there? Good. I'll be there in a minute."

"I really think you should let me out here," Brandy recalls telling him. She had begun to feel uneasy.

Lance laughed. "Look, stop worrying. Nobody's gonna hurt you."

Within minutes, he had pulled into the lot at the Hennessy Motors car dealership in Buckhead. "Okay, this is what we'll do. I've just had my other car detailed here, so it's nice and clean. I want you to take it, drive yourself to your appointment, and when you're done either drop it off back over here, or keep it overnight and drive it to the office in the morning."

"No, I can't do that. We don't even know—"

"Look, please don't do that," he said, blocking her protest with a raised hand. "You've got a license, don't you?"

"Of course, but—"

"Then just take the car, and I'll get it later," Lance insisted. "Ahhh, here it comes now."

Brandy figured she was looking at the wrong vehicle, that the sleek black Jaguar creeping toward them surely was not the one being offered to her by a complete stranger. This automobile was gorgeous, certainly too luxurious for a part-time secretary with less than twenty bucks in her purse. Lance handed her a business card. "I'm running late for a meeting," he said. "Just go. Take the car. Call me later."

Brandy recalls how seductively that pretty Jag spoke to her that afternoon, as though on its owner's behalf. She slid in behind the wheel, confused and suspicious, but as she pulled off and merged into traffic, she found herself reveling in the hum beneath her rear and the smooth burl wood gliding beneath her jittery fingertips. She turned on the stereo and heard the music of Grover Washington, a tingling piano and then a wailing saxophone clear and melodic as she descended the highway ramp. She was alone but felt as though the dialogue with brotherman big spender here had already begun, an exchange that felt quiet and safe like the floating cocoon that moved her across the miles to her doctor, who ended up telling her the obvious that afternoon: everything was fine. In fact, everything was better than fine. As she buckled herself back in and turned the key and felt the faint purring beneath her legs again, she also heard a soft ringing and saw a telephone on the console, which she had not noticed before. She decided not to answer it, but then thought it might be important, so she turned back onto the highway with Lance's phone cradled in her neck and was relieved to hear his voice, soft and knowing.

"How about lunch tomorrow?" he asked.

"Yes," she said. "Yes."

The day after loaning Brandy his Jag, Lance took her to lunch at the Coach & Six, a posh downtown restaurant popular among the power crowd, and then invited her to join him for dinner at Trader Vic's later that evening, where, in the candlelight, he shared the details of his life—that he had moved to Atlanta from New York, that he was recently divorced and owned a computer consulting firm. Mostly, though, he quizzed her on her own life, which she found refreshing in a town of male self-absorption. He applauded her pursuit of a degree in computer technology, was tickled by her adolescent tales of growing up in the Georgia sticks, and seemed genuinely flattered by her frank admission that she had never before dated a man of his status. "It's not like you think," he laughed. "I'm an underdog just like you."

Brandy was so charmed that she phoned her girlfriend later that night to begin strategizing on how to keep Lance interested in her.

"Girl, I have to figure out how to make this man need me, I mean really become his friend," she recalled saying. "You know, someone he can confide in. Why else would he need me around? I mean, really, he can get anybody to give him head." She giggled mischievously. "I mean, I can do that, too, but it won't make me special."

As it turned out, Brandy says her relationship with Lance became precisely the sexual one she was hoping to avoid. A few months into dating him, he broached the subject of a ménage à trois.

"I thought he was out of his mind, but I like sex, and I was kind of wild back then, so I agreed to try it," she said.

One night, Lance took her to a jazz club and introduced to her a handsome male friend of his, and they all left together. Their threesomes became a ritual rendezvous, so satisfying to Lance, in fact, that on some occasions he would scout among his close male and female companions for swinging companions or couples for him and Brandy.

By then, Lance's largesse had taken too strong a hold on Brandy. He tossed around lots of money, treating her to his credit card for shopping sprees at the mall, footing the entire bill, once, for a trip for her and three girlfriends to Florida for spring break. He even paid two semesters of tuition and fees for her at Emory. As repayment, in additional to making herself available, Brandy occasionally performed part-time clerical work at his home office.

She was comfortable with her trysts with Lance. In truth, Brandy says, another woman broke them apart. One afternoon, she recalled, Lance walked into his office and announced to Brandy his intention to marry Jeannine Price, whom he had met during a vacation in South America. Shortly after that, he started trotting around his pretty new fiancée and began treating Brandy as a kind of platonic pal. Brandy said that she felt so indebted to Lance that she didn't protest openly, but she resented him for it. The most painful moment was when Jeannine came rushing into the office one evening, showing off the three-carat diamond Lance had just put on her finger. "Look, Brandy, look!" she shrieked triumphantly. "Isn't it gorgeous! I've got him now, don't I?"

Brandy West says she loved Lance, not so much in a romantic way but as a friend. He was basically a good man, in her eyes, who had a dark side. Brandy could relate because she felt that she had her own dark side. She figured Lance married Jeannine because he needed a certain type of woman on his arm. Jeannine was a trophy, could cook and clean, and said all the right things. Brandy, on the other hand, was too much like Lance.

chapter ten

GOLD DIGGERS

Clint is sitting in the airy dining room of Paschal's, freshly painted and remodeled from its humbler days as a favorite soul food haunt and meeting ground in the late 1950s and early '60s for civil rights activists. It is lunchtime, and his plate is piled high; fried chicken, collard greens, macaroni and cheese, and candied yams. He gulps down some iced tea. "Lance Herndon *loved* some women. And guess what? The women *loved* some Lance, too. Most would have gone to the end of the earth for that man."

It is obvious that Clint Rucker doesn't find Lance's private life nearly as objectionable as Detective Anastasio, who frowns and shakes his head whenever the subject of Lance and women is mentioned. Clint's explanation for this is that while he doesn't condone such promiscuity, Lance was less a womanizer than a man who enjoyed a unique understanding with several women. Clint likened the arrangement to an Arab sheik whose family portrait might include a bevy of women with whom the patriarch is intimate. Lance's women were very much aware of the fact that their relationships with him were not exclusive. Until his death, at least, they all could smile—each of them was getting what they wanted out of the relationship. Lance had rules, and any woman who dealt with him knew what those rules were. She also knew that if she played by them, Lance was very generous and would give her anything she wanted or needed. They really believed that about him, and he never let them down.

This was not entirely true, of course. As Detective Anastasio was learning, Lance's carousing had turned finding his killer into a kind of sexual Rubik's cube. A few days after Lance was killed, Jeannine Herndon had sat in a metal chair across from Anastasio's desk at the Roswell Police Department to provide more background on her ex-husband. She was still numb from the news. Anastasio turned the conversation to the subject of Jeannine's relationship to Herndon.

"So what actually broke up your marriage to Lance?" he asked.

Jeannine admitted, somewhat hesitantly, that her marriage to Lance had failed because he had routinely cheated on her. It had become clear early on in their marriage that the man had some serious problems with commitment. She had long suspected Lance of cheating; then in 1989 Lance's assistant Zonya had come across some nude photos in Lance's desk and, feeling sorry for Jeannine, handed them over to her. At the time, the singer Gary Jenkins was Zonya's fiancée, so Zonya was sensitive about the challenges of having a man who traveled a lot and was desired by many women. Lance was not in the pictures, but seeing them destroyed Jeannine's trust in their marriage. Making matters worse was that the photos were of Lacey Banks, one of Lance's part-time employees, whom Jeannine had to see frequently working in their home office. She later found out that Lance even had encounters with Lacey in their bedroom. Jeannine confronted Lance about it, and he agreed to seek counseling with her.

Jeannine was working as a flight attendant then, so she was traveling quite a bit and just didn't feel she could ever trust Lance again. She was right: shortly after they moved onto Bluffview Trace and she gave birth to Harrison, Jeannine caught Lance in an affair with his secretary, Natasha. She and the baby moved out for eighteen months, while she went with Lance to counseling in hopes of working through their problems. But when Jeannine and Harrison moved back, she realized Lance hadn't changed a bit, and that he was still sneaking around on her. Jeannine could not stomach the infidelity anymore. She filed for divorce.

In the end, Detective Anastasio decided that he liked Jeannine Herndon, felt sorry for her. Sure, the ex-wife always makes for a natural suspect in murder cases such as this. And the fact that Lance had cheated on her during their entire marriage could qualify as motive, he supposed, as well as the fact that she knew the code to the house security alarm. But several other factors, in his view, automatically disqualified her as a suspect. For instance, Anastasio had checked out Lance's life insurance policy, which was valued at $850,000. Her alimony agreement was for some five grand a month until their son turned eighteen. Their kid, Harrison, was four years old, meaning Lance would have paid out at least $840,000, on top of the extra cash payments of $10,000 each he had agreed to pay Jeannine over the next couple of years to help her get back on her feet, as per their divorce settlement. Based on the straight arithmetic, plus the fact that Lance had proven to be a fairly committed father to their son, Anastasio figured that Jeannine Herndon had more to gain from her ex alive than dead. On top of all that, her alibi for that night squared. Anastasio had gone over and talked to her boyfriend, Thomas Patterson, checked his phone records, and it appeared as if he and Jeannine were, in fact, at her apartment at the time Herndon was likely murdered. Jeannine had wanted Patterson to spend the night, but he had ended up going home fairly late. He called her from his place, and then made some other calls.

Anastasio asked Jeannine whether she was familiar with any of the women Lance may have been dating recently. She replied that, knowing Lance, it could be any number of women. The only two whose names she heard recently were Kathi and Dionne. She didn't know their last names, although Zonya and Holly certainly should. And of course, knowing Lance, Lacey Banks was probably still somewhere in his life.

At his core, Anastasio considers himself a fairly conservative man. It does not matter that as a teenager, he wore his hair long, dreamed of playing guitar in a rock band, and dropped out of high school before going back and earning his GED (eventually he enrolled in college and graduated with a bachelor's degree in criminal justice). It does not matter either that he is in his third marriage, or that he curses incessantly. In his own view—despite a lifetime of appearing radical at times or just plain antisocial at others, Anastasio prides himself on maintaining a solidly upright code of conduct. "Here you have this man, Lance, who was successful in some circles but who was so unsuccessful in his personal life," he says. "Jeannine would have gone with him to the end of the earth, even if he had been penniless. But all he did was play around on her. It's hard to respect a man like that. I just felt sorry for him. He fucked his life up."

———

Jacques Albright, the successful Atlanta oncologist and Lance's best friend, is a handsome man, sharp-featured with dark, brooding eyes. After Lance's death, rumors surrounding Lance's sexuality caused some problems between him and his wife, he tells me. "Lance and I hung out together so much that my wife had some hard questions for me. I was a little pissed off, but I understood her concern. But Lance, as far as I ever knew, was only into women. That's it. And we talked about women a lot." Jacques laughs. "I mean, I've made the mistake before of assuming a guy was into women when he wasn't. I remember years ago, I had a friend who I discovered was gay, and at first I was shocked and felt somewhat betrayed because we'd had all these conversations about women. But when I really thought back on it, it dawned on me that in all those conversations, *I* had been the one doing all the talking about women. That was never the case with Lance."

Jacques Albright says he was introduced to Lance at an art gallery in late 1979, and they became fast friends—mostly as a result of Lance following up on that initial meeting. Lance always made it a point to stay in touch, engaging Jacques in conversations about the local business scene and apprising him of happenings big and small on the social circuit. "There are a lot of ways to enter the scene here," he says, "and you've got to figure out the one that's best suited to your personality and your goals. When I came into town, I reached out to the old guard of black physicians and joined their organizations, and I got to meet a lot of them so that when I started my practice, they supported me. Referrals are an important part of my business, and I'm black, so I knew I needed to go to the well to meet black doctors. One of the misconceptions people have in moving here is that opportunity just falls from the sky. But you have to have a skill and mindset about doing something—it's not just going to come to you.

"When Lance came to Atlanta he was, I would say, under the radar screen. He moved out to Alpharetta, which was on the other side of the world to most professional blacks here. I live downtown; Atlanta has changed, but even back then blacks resided in areas other than southwest Atlanta. Lance was out there even before it became in vogue to live in Alpharetta. The statement that it made was that he was his own person, and that maybe he wasn't overt, but more covert in his marketing of himself. But what made Lance stand out was what I would call his efficiencies in building relationships. Because he was into computers, he really used that technology to help him keep a lot of order in his relationships. He was always in touch with people, made them feel like they were important and on his mind. He had these huge databases, and whenever he would travel, he would send cards to clients, and he had software that would remind him to send their kids birthday cards or whatever. And so people appreciated him as being conscientious. Lance *always* had my back. He would call and say, 'Hey you need tickets to anything? You need this, you need that?' He just had the contacts. So if I needed tickets to something, I'd tell him, and he'd say, 'I'll make it happen,' and boom, he did. I remember he'd always say, 'When we get our first snow, I'm going to get the plane and we'll go on down to the Bahamas.' That's how he was."

As their mutual friend Ken Crooks confirmed, Jacques says it was Lance's generosity that made him such a beloved figure among women. If the city's teeming climate of attractive, single black women has bred a culture of tightwad bachelors, Lance Herndon's role as a sugar daddy made him a magnet to women who appreciated big spenders. "Lance made women feel very good for the most part. But their level of importance was more in their minds than in his view of them. He wasn't one of those guys who had a bunch of lines to give them. He was pretty much blunt and to the point. But he was also gentlemanly to them. If they needed something, he'd get it for them, make sure it happened for them. He was always attentive to them, but in a very expedient manner.

"The only woman I know that Lance really cared about is Jeannine," he says. "I remember once we were standing in his kitchen; that was always my favorite part of the house because it always smelled so good in there when they were married. Jeannine was always cooking something good. But by then, she had left Lance, and we were standing there, and he got really quiet and admitted to me how much he wanted her back. He told me he'd give up everything he had to have his family back."

In characterizing the women his best friend dated, Jacques Albright does not equivocate. "Gold diggers," he says. "That's all they were."

chapter eleven

HOUSE CALLS

When Kathi Collins came sashaying into Anastasio's office nearly a week after the murder, Anastasio could not help but notice what appeared to be a visible lack of grief. If Kathi harbored any anguish, it seemed to be focused on her wardrobe—or rather the portion of it still locked up in Lance's home. Kathi spent the first few minutes of her interview with Anastasio fussing about the Roswell Police Department denying her access into Herndon's house to retrieve her garments, which, she pointed out, did not belong to the Herndon estate and therefore ought to be released without the hassle.

With all the patience that he could muster, Detective Anastasio assured Kathi that he would return her belongings as soon as possible, that the officers were moving as fast as they could, but that the bedroom was still designated a crime scene, which meant that nothing could leave. This, Kathi insisted, was nonsense, considering that those things belonged to her, and that she could be in and out of the house in no time flat and then the officers could get back to doing whatever it was they were still doing in there.

Pushing ahead, Anastasio reminded Kathi Collins that in her initial statement to Detective Evans, she said that around the time of Lance's death she had been out of town at a funeral in Houston and had returned on the evening of August 7.

Yes, that's correct, Kathi told him, tossing back her long silky hair in a display of impatience. This was a habit that had always annoyed Lance. It annoyed Anastasio, too.

Kathi went on to explain that she and her niece, Cassandra Collins, had flown back to Atlanta on the seventh, after the funeral. Cassandra was from Seattle and visited Kathi during the Olympics. Lance had taken Kathi to the opening ceremonies, and had given her and Cassandra tickets to a few events, including the U.S. women's basketball championship in which they won the gold medal.

Rummaging through her designer handbag, Kathi handed over several receipts, which verified her whereabouts on the night of the seventh—a boarding pass from Southwest Flight 476, an airport parking receipt, and a receipt for gas. She told Anastasio that she and Cassandra had gone to dinner at a restaurant called Embers over on Roswell Road where the food was to die for; she and Lance ate there all the time. She was able to provide a dinner receipt as well. She and her niece dined for a few hours. This sparked Anastasio's curiosity.

"Why, after having been out of town," he asked, "didn't you call Mr. Herndon or go by to see him?"

Kathi told him that she had paged Lance around nine or nine-fifteen with the restaurant's number, and that Lance had called right back. The bartender received the call and gave her the phone. They didn't talk for very long, nor did they discuss getting together that evening, due to the fact that Lance's grandmother was visiting from Virginia. The Embers receipt indicated that Kathi Collins paid her bill at 11:15. She says she went straight home and made a few phone calls. One was to a girlfriend who lived in Houston. That call lasted about thirty minutes, and then she made another call to her mother back in Seattle, to whom she spoke for about forty minutes.

"And that's it?" Anastasio asked.

Kathi's expression turned sheepish. She admitted to having phoned one other person.

His name was Hayden Eastman, a new male acquaintance of hers whom she had met a couple of months earlier. She made arrangements to go over and spend the night with him. He lived out in Duluth. If necessary, she told the detective, Hayden would be able to corroborate her presence at his home that night, and so would his friend, Fred Bey, who was at Hayden's home as well, fixing Hayden's computer. Kathi said she went to bed shortly after arriving at Hayden's, and that he joined her a little later, after Fred left.

In closing, Anastasio asked her whether she was in possession of any of Mr. Herndon's credit cards. Kathi handed over Lance Herndon's Wachovia Visa. She said her last charges on it were her airline ticket to Houston, and gas on the day she got back in town. And yes, she had used it just one other time recently: a couple of weeks ago, she had gotten a manicure. She had charged that to Lance's card, too.

Several days later, the Roswell Police Department received a letter from Kathi.

Kathi L. Collins
3502 Harbor Pt. Pky
Atlanta, Georgia 30350
(770) 604-9708

August 14, 1996

Memo to: Detective M.B. Evans
City of Roswell Police Dept.
And the Executors of the
Estate of Lance H. Herndon.

re: request for property from the Lance H. Herndon home.

The following is a list as best I can recall of clothing and other
items in the home. Some clothing items may not be specifically
listed because I would have to go through my three closets at
home to determine every item that is at the Herndon home.
I would appreciate this matter being handled as soon as
possible.

List of Property:
- black knit Tadashi skirt suit
- red knit evening skirt and top
- white with gold IIF dinner suit
- green and turquoise shorts and jacket by Forwear
- orange Yasaman jacket
- peach Votre Nom silk blouse
- peach Votre Nom stirrup pants

- black knit skirt by Ginger

- bronze sheer blouse by Liz Claiborne

- bronze/tan camisole

- black 3-piece skirt suit by Yasaman/Ronet

- purple 2-piece skirt suit

- black double-breasted dress

- black cashmere dress

- black jeans (2 pair with belts)

- asst. tops & T-shirts with jeans

- ivory turtle neck sweater

- ivory Votre Nom stirrup pants

- ivory & beige fox fur piece 6–8 ft. long

- black silk raincoat by Panache

- asst. other clothing items mixed in with all of these items
  on my side of Lance's closet

- undergarments and—shirts on the rack above my clothing
  items hanging in the closet

- black suede North Beach leather jacket hanging
  on Lance's side of the closet (receipt for this jacket
  is attached)

- in the master bedroom, the counter to your right, the far
  left drawer and the cabinet under the drawer; all contents
  of this drawer and cabinet are mine

- the purple perfume bottle on top of this counter is mine

- bottle of Zhivago 24 carat cologne

- framed photograph of me on Lance's dresser in master
  bedroom

- two Bermuda T-shirts with a bright colorful carnival mask; silk screened and the words Carnival and Bermuda

- silver and black bikini top by Carabella Collections that we recently ordered via mail and should be in the envelope it was delivered in, either in the office or upstairs

- Georgio Armani double/lens glasses in a leather Armani case (they should be in the Porsche)

- photos and negative of me and my niece at the Women's Gold basketball game for the Olympics on August 4, if Holly has not taken this film to develop it should still be in the camera

- photos and negatives of me and my friend Teresa at the Olympic track and field events

- photos and negatives of me and Lance at the Olympic opening ceremony

- photos and negatives of me and Lance during our trip to Greece and Egypt June 1996

- all other photos and video of me and me and Lance

- bottles of Shafer Merlot

As proof that the merlot wine belonged to her, Kathi Collins attached a copy of a June 19, 1996, e-mail from Holly Steuber to Mr. Herndon regarding Steuber's difficulty locating the brand in stores.

This is an e-mail transmission Lance gave me informing me of the disposition of Merlot he buys for my consumption only. All bottles of Merlot were purchased for me.

———

Lacey Banks, the last person to see Lance alive, hired an attorney to escort her to Detective Anastasio's office for questioning. This, along with her nervous manner that day, had the effect of whetting the detective's suspicions. Considering that he hadn't yet identified Miss Banks as a suspect, he could not see the need for an attorney. He wondered what she was hiding. She had, in fact, spent part of the evening before his murder with Herndon, and while she had cooperated a few days before by coming into the lab to provide fingerprints and hair samples, of late she had seemed to be avoiding investigators.

"You're a hard woman to getta hold of, Miss Banks," Anastasio said.

Lacey's attorney, an officious white man named George Greenwood, explained that Miss Banks had retained him because the Roswell PD was harassing her, or at least it sure felt like harassment to her. They were calling her at her job at a local furniture store, and had even showed up at her home one morning, banging on her door. Their aggression was frightening.

Such measures seemed unnecessarily pushy unless Ms. Banks was a suspect in the murder, Counsel Greenwood said. Anastasio told him that at this point she was merely a witness, but his men had been frustrated in their attempts to locate her for further questioning.

Anastasio fired off a battery of questions, and Lacey Banks volleyed back. She had known Mr. Herndon for about ten or twelve years, working for him off and on during that time in administrative roles—typing, filing, mailing out letters, general clerical work. Their relationship was unique, complicated; it had changed back and forth from intimate to platonic over the years. But they were always friends, no matter what was going on between them.

Lacey admitted to Anastasio that she had been sexually involved with Lance recently, though she couldn't exactly recall the last time they had slept together. She was certain that she didn't sleep with Lance on Wednesday night or Thursday morning. After working at his home that Wednesday night, she drove straight home, where she remained for the rest of the night, until she left for work the following morning.

She did note, however, that when she got home from Lance's that night, there was a message from him on her answering machine, and she called him back that night. She was sure phone records would confirm this. Anastasio wanted to know what Lance's message to her was. It was just Lance joking around, she told the detective, asking her to consider marrying him. But he wasn't serious, he never was.

"Lance and I always played around like that," Lacey said. "As I said, we were close."

Anastasio was curious: "What did Mr. Herndon say when you called him back? How did he sound? Was there any indication that something was wrong?"

"No, not really. He sounded fine, fairly relaxed. And I told him I made it home okay and we said good night."

Who is Jimmy "Sweet" Turner, Anastastio wanted to know, and what financial relationship did he have with Mr. Herndon? Lacey told him that Sweet was her ex-boyfriend, but she did not share the whole sordid story with him.

She kept to herself how she had been charmed nearly a year ago by this tall, dark-skinned man, a rakish bad boy—"preacher flashy" is how she later described him to me. He had slicked-back hair and deep dimples boring toward a perfectly white smile. Within a couple of months after meeting him, Lacey was so smitten that she cosigned for him on a used Jaguar and let him move into her home. Only later did she learn that the man had a wife and a couple of kids back home in Detroit. She did not tell Anastasio, either, how she had discovered her new lover's double life when he was arrested and locked up in Texas for violating his parole on drug charges. It was during his incarceration that she went through his pockets and files and saw pictures of his family. Months later, upon his release, Lacey confronted him, and there was a fight in which she hit her head against a wall and he pounced on her and would not let her up. He moved out after the incident.

As far as a financial relationship between Lance and Sweet, there really wasn't one to speak of, Lacey said. There was a time Sweet could not pay—in fact he was in prison—the car note on the Jaguar. To avoid Lacey's credit being ruined, Lance had loaned Sweet about five thousand dollars, and kept the vehicle as collateral. But Sweet had paid him back, and that was that. Anyway, Sweet had been in California for the past three weeks. Anastasio asked whether Sweet was ever bothered by the fact that she was sleeping with Lance. Lacey answered that Sweet didn't know that she and Lance were intimate.

"And how can you be so sure of that?" the detective asked pointedly.

To this, Lacey could only shrug.

N ot having made much headway, Detective Anastasio returned to the crime scene the following day and spoke with Zonya Adams. She was working alone in the Access suite, which had been ransacked during the investigators' scrutiny. Papers were strewn across the floor, folders sagged from file cabinets, cassette tapes littered the desks. Zonya told Anastasio that despite her boss's death, the firm was still trying to honor all its business contracts. For the time being, Jeannine, along with Zonya and Lance's mother, were running the business until the firm's contractual obligations to clients were met. In truth, though, there was really not much of a company, no Access Inc. to speak of, without Lance. Lance *was* the business.

"Were you and Mr. Herndon ever intimate?"

Zonya told Anastasio that she had never been romantically involved with Mr. Herndon. Lance was simply a dear friend. In fact, she had recently gotten married and was the mother of a baby girl. Zonya said she was aware that Lance was dating at least two women at the time he was killed, Kathi Collins and Dionne Baugh. She knew Kathi best because she was Lance's main girlfriend, the woman with whom he always made his public appearances. Kathi was a bit on the snooty side, but she was really okay once you got to know her. She spent quite a bit of time at the house, lots of overnights with Lance. She had a whole closet full of clothes hanging up in one of his bedroom closets.

Zonya said Lance generally had relationships with a ridiculous number of women, and they were all in a constant state of flux. Of late, he had stopped trusting Kathi because on occasion she wasn't where she said she was going to be, which bothered him. He would walk around the office saying that he was going to "fire" Kathi soon. He even hired a private investigator to check on her, see what she was up to. But Kathi was out of town when Lance was killed, or was just getting back. Besides, Zonya added, she just couldn't imagine Kathi doing anything like that.

"What can you tell me about Lacey Banks?" Anastasio asked.

"I really don't know her that well," Zonya said.

Zonya explained that she had started working for Lance about six years ago, and that Lacey had worked for him long before then—though what exactly she did, Zonya wasn't sure. Lacey had resurfaced a few weeks ago and was doing some part-time clerical work for Lance, mostly on Wednesday nights. Lance told Zonya that Lacey was having some financial problems, and that he was helping her out by giving her some administrative work on the side. Zonya assumed that Lance must have been paying Lacey out of his pocket because one of Zonya's jobs was handling payroll, and she had never cut a check to Lacey. She thought Lance had an odd relationship with Lacey. He always looked out for her, did her lots of favors. She had this boyfriend, a real hustler type named Sweet Turner, who was always in debt for something or another. Once she had Lance loan Sweet some money, and Lance kept the guy's car as collateral. It was weird seeing this other man's car just sitting there in Lance's driveway for weeks. Then one day, the car disappeared. Zonya figured Sweet must've paid the money back. Or maybe he didn't, and Lance sold the thing. In any event, Lance never mentioned it again, and Zonya never asked.

"So tell me some more about this Dionne woman. Who is she?"

Lance started out really into Dionne, Zonya said, but of late he was cooling off on her. She worked as a secretary or something over at MARTA, or the Metropolitan Atlanta Rapid Transit Authority, and went to school part-time at Georgia State. She knew this only because Dionne was always borrowing the office laptop to do her homework. Lance must have loaned it to her before all this happened, because Zonya couldn't find the computer anywhere. The man even bought Dionne a Mercedes—which she was still driving after his death. But Dionne was a pushy type, and that was starting to get on Lance's nerves. Just a week or so ago, he started calling her a "crazy bitch" to Zonya and spoke of ending the relationship. One confrontation had occurred a couple of months ago when Dionne came over to the house late one night and caught Lance with Kathi. There had been a big fuss over that, which ended with Lance calling the police. It was really quite a ruckus, and left some bad feelings in the air. Zonya said she believed Dionne might have even been arrested for trespassing that night. She had heard Lance mention something about an upcoming court date.

For whatever it was worth, Jeannine Herndon had also called Anastasio with a story. She and Lance had a friend named Eva Allen. Lance was the godfather to Eva's children. Incidentally, Eva had been in touch with a psychic over the past few years and had been floored by the woman's premonitions. A few years back, the psychic insisted that Eva would give birth to twins. At the time, Eva was struggling to even get pregnant. A sonogram a few months later proved the psychic right. In any case, Eva had called Jeannine the other day to recount an eerie visit with her psychic. Without any knowledge over what had happened to Lance, the psychic said, "You're upset over a murder. And the person who did this is someone new in the victim's life. The victim has only known this person for three months. They are very controlling and motivated by money, either money they felt was owed to them, or actually was owed to them."

Zonya's statement—and even Jeannine's odd tale—took Anastasio's mind back to his first encounter with Dionne. It made him recall how strangely she had behaved when he and his partner Marty Evans went to interview her. It was the evening Herndon's body was discovered, and Anastasio and Evans went by her house in Norcross. They knocked on the door, and nobody answered, so they walked away and spoke to a woman who lived across the street. They asked her whether she knew Miss Baugh, and when she said she did, Anastasio gave her his card and told her to have Miss Baugh call him. Then he and Evans got back in the car and drove away. A couple of minutes later, Anastasio's cell phone rang. It was the neighbor telling him Baugh had just come over to her house to ask what the cops wanted. Baugh had told her that she hadn't heard them knocking on the door because she was in the shower. But, the neighbor went on, this was strange, considering Baugh's face was all made up, and she was wearing a business suit. Baugh then got in her car and drove away, the neighbor said.

Anastasio and his partner drove back over there, parked right in front of her house, and waited. A few minutes later Baugh drove up in her silver Mercedes and pulled into her driveway. When Anastasio and Evans got out of the car, she started running toward the house and then collapsed on the ground, crying hysterically. She said she had just found out from her aunt or somebody that Herndon was dead. But Anastasio noticed that in all that hysterical sobbing and carrying on, he didn't see one tear in her eyes. She invited Anastasio into her home and said that Lance had come by her home the night before to drop off the office laptop computer. He asked to spend the night, but she wasn't in the mood, she said. She was a marketing major at Georgia State University and had plenty of studying to catch up on. Besides, she had just dropped her four-year-old daughter, along with her husband, at the airport—they lived in Jamaica—and she was feeling a bit depressed. But even as she offered her alibi—that she was at home alone on the night Herndon was killed—Anastasio felt strangely unsettled by the woman.

This weird encounter, though, was not enough to erase Detective Anastasio's doubts about Kathi Collins and Lacey Banks. Their alibis were hardly foolproof. The phone records trotted out by both women only proved that calls had been placed to Lance Herndon's home but did not—could not—prove that either women actually did the calling. Kathi had said she paged Herndon from the Embers restaurant where she was dining with her niece and that Herndon called her back, reaching her at the restaurant bar. The phone records backed up this version, at least to the point of showing a call from Lance's house to the restaurant. Kathi's dinner receipt showed her paying the bill shortly before midnight. But until Lance's precise time of death was known, this left open the remote possibility that Kathi would have had enough time to travel the couple of miles to Bluffview Trace and back to the restaurant that night. If Zonya's story about Kathi catching Lance cheating held up, that would serve as enough of a motive to at least merit deeper scrutiny of Kathi.

Lacey Banks, for her part, was the last person to see Lance Herndon alive. She had left Herndon's home that night at around 10:30 P.M., she said, and phone records appeared to support her statement that a conversation with Lance an hour later from her apartment was her last contact with him. The blood and pubic hair samples she provided to investigators did not match those found at the murder scene. But if Lacey wasn't present at the murder scene and didn't seem to have an obvious motive, her boyfriend Sweet Turner conceivably could have been jealous of Lacey's affair with Lance. The problem was that Anastasio had been unable to track down Sweet Turner, who apparently had moved to California months ago.

Following up on Zonya's lead that Dionne Baugh had been arrested for trespassing, Detective Anastasio caught up with Officer Tommy Williams later that evening. Williams recounted the tale of a bizarre July domestic dispute at the Herndon residence. He was on regular street patrol about a month back when the dispatcher asked him to go check out a disturbance over at 9060 Bluffview Trace. He drove over to the subdivision of Northcliff, off Riverside Road, and pulled up to this big house, which was looking fairly tame, as far he could see. There was a gray Mercedes parked in the driveway, and he walked past it and started browsing around the property to check things out. He wasn't sure why, but something in his head told him to turn back and look in that car, and he's glad he did, because he spotted this woman in the back, lying on the car floorboard, hiding under a pile of clothes. It was strange as shit. He shone his flashlight on her, and the lady got out, yelling and screaming and calling him everything but the child of God. He calmed her down long enough for her to tell him that her boyfriend lived in this house, but he wouldn't open the door. She told him she was a college student, she had an exam coming, her books were in the house, and she needed them badly. Williams called the dispatcher and asks her to phone the owner of the house and tell him there was an officer outside. Could he please come to the door so they could settle this—get the lady her books, and that would be the end of it. Seconds later the dispatcher called the officer back and told him the owner refused to come to the door. Now, Williams had no option but to ask this woman to leave the premises, because unless she could verify her story, she was technically trespassing. She refused to leave, got all pissed off again, and started hollering something about the car, the Mercedes, and how he bought it for her. That might be true, Officer Williams told her, but the man didn't want her on his property. She refused to leave, so he was forced to get his cuffs out and arrest her. The woman refused to be cuffed and fought him something terrible as he was putting her in the squad car. She was totally combative, just way out of control. And to think, the whole incident could have been avoided if this asshole had just come to the door and brought the woman her books.

That afternoon, Anastasio sat in his office and listened to four exchanges between Lance and the Roswell 911 dispatcher.

———

With his girlfriend Kathi frightened in bed, Lance slips away down into his office to alert police of a disturbance at his home. He makes the first call just before midnight, July 9, 1996.

> *Roswell 911.*
>
> *Hey, there's a, somebody knocking at my door, in the middle of the night.*
>
> *Yeah, it is the middle of the night. What's the address? 9060 Bluffview Trace?*
>
> *Right.*
>
> *You weren't expecting anyone, I take it, from out of town or anything.*
>
> *No.*
>
> *Okay.*
>
> *Yeah, and uh, the deal on that is that it might be like an ex-girlfriend or whatever . . .*
>
> *Mm-mmm . . .*
>
> *That's giving me some problems, and . . . So whoever it is, they just need to go away.*
>
> *Do you know if it's a male or female?*
>
> *I don't know. But I'm just saying there's nobody that I'm expecting. So whoever it is, they just need to go away.*
>
> *Okay, what's your last name?*
>
> *Herndon.*
>
> *And your first name?*
>
> *Lance.*
>
> *We'll send somebody out there and have them leave the premises. Okay?*
>
> *Okay.*

More than five hours later, at 5:40 A.M., July 10, Herndon calls
911 again.

Roswell 911.

*Hi. This is Lance Herndon. Unfortunately, I had the plea-
sure of calling you guys last night.*

Mm-mm.

*Okay. I guess when I like wake up and the light comes up
I will get what they call a restraining order. Is that what you
get for people that you want to . . .*

Yes, you can.

*Um, and, in the meanwhile, I'm between a rock and a
hard place. Here's the scoop. Um, I go out there and confront
this woman and she is like whacko. Um, and I have to protect
myself. You're gonna have a bigger problem than just getting
somebody away from my door. So, and I'm being very honest
with you. I hate to keep bothering you, but if I take it into my
own hands it could get interesting. So, and then last night
they said something to the effect that well this is a domestic.
They can't get involved. I mean, what do you kind of want
me to do?*

*It's not that we can't get involved. It's just that we need
all parties to cooperate. You called for us to help you. She's
telling us she has your car. We needed you to come out and tell
our officer "That is not my car," or "That is my car," and
settle it from there. We're just hearing one side of it at a time
and it doesn't work that way.*

I understand, but I mean, it's kind of like my house, okay?

I understand that.

*Okay. And somebody is like banging on doors, and kick-
ing things at five in the morning.*

We asked her to leave and apparently she left because our officer would not have left and left her standing there on your doorstep. Is she back?

Yeah. She's back right now.

Okay, we'll send them back out there.

I mean, I know you heard her side of the story, and I got no problem with that. I know you get this sort of problem all the time, but when people kick people's doors at twelve, and then they kick 'em again at five in the morning . . . you kind of say to yourself one side seems really kind of weird, like why would they keep doing that?

I understand. When our officer gets there I'm going to call you so that you can go meet with the officer.

I don't know that I want to meet with anybody. Um, maybe I should call my attorney, and maybe try to figure this out another way 'cause I'm, I'm not, I'm thinking that I don't have to do anything more than what I'm doing, and that a person is just, you know semi-stalking me, so what, I don't understand why I have to look at them and go "Oh, that's them," you know.

Is it her car she has?

Um, it's very complicated, but it's her car. It's registered in my name, but she pays the note on it.

Okay, so the car belongs to you. If it's registered in your name you are the owner of that car. She is basically telling us the truth when she says she has your car, and that's where we're stuck. Okay?

But, I understand that, but by the same token, ma'am, um, I'm thinking that because she has my car doesn't give you the ability to beat my house at five in the morning. You see what I'm saying?

We're stuck in the middle here, and I hate to, you know I don't want to be ugly about it, but you're both being very hard to get along with. Okay, well, when I dispatch this out, I'm gonna tell the officer you do not want to meet with him, and he's gonna have to take it from there. But if he tells me to call you, Lance, I'm gonna have to call you.

All right. All right.

A few minutes later, at 5:53 A.M., the Roswell Police Department calls Herndon.

Mr. Herndon?

Yes.

This is Joyce from Roswell PD.

Yes.

They've asked me for a couple of things. What is her name?

Dionne Baugh.

Okay, our officer wants to make it clear that if she refuses to leave, we're gonna have to arrest her.

That's fine.

Five minutes later, at 5:58 A.M., July 10, the police call Herndon a final time.

Mr. Herndon?

Yes.

Roswell PD again. Dionne states that you called her. And see, this is what we get in the middle of when you won't . . .

I'm sorry, ma'am. Well, she just won't leave the house.

Did you call her and ask her to come back over there?

Well that would be so crazy, ma'am, to call somebody to come here and then call you.

Well, it happens.

I can't believe that a police officer asked her to leave and she won't. Is that what's occurring? She's got to be kidding.

It happens all the time.

Well, here's the scoop. I just want, I mean I'm not trying to see anybody hurt. I just want to be left alone. If she could just leave. That would be perfect. Do you see what I'm saying?

They're dealing with it the best they can.

I'll get the restraining order as soon as the light comes up.

At 6:03, Roswell police call and alert Roswell Detention that Dionne Baugh is in custody and en route.

Roswell Detention.

Um, female on the way.

Okay.

And she is pretty hysterical right now. I don't think she's out of control, but she's pretty well shook up.

Okay.

Stupid people, stupid people.

chapter twelve

FOREIGN AFFAIRS

It is around noon when the taxi driver, a middle-aged Jamaican guy sporting a wide straw hat, pulls up in front of the Montego Bay Ritz-Carlton. The driver's high-wattage smile dims and then disappears as he peers down at the address, miles across the countryside and off the tourist circuit.

Nearly an hour later, in a large office in downtown Montego Bay, a wealthy real estate developer is willing to talk to me about Dionne Baugh, even though he fears being singled out as a traitor by Dionne Baugh's father-in-law, Edward Nelson, patriarch of one of Jamaica's most prominent families. "Jamaicans are very tight knit and very proud," he tells me in a rolling Caribbean accent. "You're not going to get us to say very much about each other."

The developer is a tall man, fair-skinned, with brown curly hair. For someone who owns a sizable portion of the island's commercial real estate, his attire is decidedly low-key; island casual in a short-sleeve cotton shirt flecked with tiny sailboats, a pair of khakis, and sandals. "We're protective that way," he goes on. "Most people—I mean African Americans—don't understand this about us. We can be very guarded about certain things. Most tend to interpret this as arrogance." He chuckles. "I don't know how true it is, but I've heard it said that during the Middle Passage, those Africans who gave the white slave traders the most problems en route to America never quite made it all the way, but were dropped off here on the island. They figured we'd be too difficult to tame."

The tale seems somewhat contrary to historical fact. When Christopher Columbus arrived on the island back in the late 1400s, he encountered a bunch of Indians, or Arawaks as they were called, who he considered to be savage and ignorant. He marveled over their well-built physiques and coarse hair, and their peaceful disposition. But over the next century, as Europeans began inhabiting the island with their cattle and horses, these Arawaks started dying due to disease. The Spanish increasingly settled the island, bringing their African slaves with them, but in the mid-1600s English military forces broke Spain's weak hold on the Caribbean and, for the next two centuries, exploited the island's robust sugar crop, which became a boon to traders. The plantations were controlled by British landowners and manned by rising numbers of black slaves captured and shipped out of West Africa. Jamaica remained a British colony for the next 300 years, or until 1962, when it became independent. Whether or not the hostile Africans wound up in Negril or New Orleans, the saga of black Jamaicans seems too similar to that of African Americans for much proud hair-splitting.

The real estate developer was not acquainted with Dionne, but was an associate of her husband, Shawn's. He describes Shawn as a gentleman, from an upper-class family. His father is a good man, an engineer, and his mother is quite a woman herself. She's white, a schoolteacher from Britain. They met while he was studying in Scotland.

Shawn Peter Nelson, in the late spring of 1988, met Dionne Baugh on the dance floor of a Miami nightclub called the Hungry Whale and wound up in a relationship that quickly turned serious. Back then what Shawn liked most about Dionne, besides her liberated sexuality, was her drive and sense of independence. A naturalized American citizen originally from Kingston, Dionne had moved to Miami years ago with her family. She was living comfortably as a bachelorette in a two-bedroom apartment when he met her, attending community college part-time and working as a bank secretary. Shawn, a native of Montego Bay, Jamaica, was residing in Miami on a student visa while he studied for his pilot's license. He not only appreciated the hospitality Dionne lavished on him, from the home-cooked Jamaican meals, boiled green bananas and dumplings and Johnnie cakes, to the frequent invitations to spend nights in her lively bed, but also grew to believe her assertion that he would never find a mate more perfect for him. By May 1990 the couple had married, and Dionne was pregnant with Amanda.

Marital strife came early. It is the opinion of some who know Shawn that his new wife had grown accustomed to slick American men, high-rolling double-breasted types who lived on credit cards and get-rich schemes. That was not Shawn at all. Beneath his ruggedly handsome looks, the chiseled bronze face and long, sinewy physique, beat the heart of a dove. The son of Edward Nelson, the well-regarded civil engineer and member of the Jamaican Parlia-

ment, Shawn was raised to be not a fighter but a gentleman, his aris-
tocratic blood rendering him a mellow soul. The private schools
and maids and nannies had insulated him from third-world hard-
ness, preserved his baby-soft hands and dreamy eyes. Shawn had
but two humble goals in life: to fly commercial jets, and to start
a family.

Dionne was born to working-class folks in the island's tough
capital of Kingston. If she started out impressed by her husband's
lofty Jamaican birthright, he says, she came to resent its impracti-
cality on foreign soil. Shortly after they married, she began to chas-
tise Shawn for what she perceived as a lack of fierce ambition and a
subtle air of entitlement. His plans to complete aviation training
and move them back to Jamaica struck her as small-minded.

The Jamaican developer shakes his head, as though in pity for
Shawn. He rises from his desk, stretching out his legs, and steps out
of the office, returning moments later with two Coca-Colas.

"I think their problems started once they moved to Atlanta," he
continues. "He moved there to further his pilot's training, I believe.
She was taking college classes, too. But when I looked up, Shawn
was back in Montego Bay. I figured something was wrong, because
their daughter Amanda was back here too."

Indeed, Dionne proved to be a moody spouse; one moment she
could be sweet and calm and affectionate to him and Amanda, and
the next wickedly cruel and selfish. On her worst days, her studies,
her comfort, and her own livelihood seemed to matter most, and it
was her tirades to that effect that eventually drove a wedge between
them. Feeling like an albatross around her neck, and growing in-
creasingly wary of her dual persona, Shawn suggested that he and
Amanda move back to Jamaica to his parents' home while she fin-
ished school and figured out whether she wanted the marriage to

work. He was not surprised when Dionne agreed that such an arrangement would be best for all of them.

Until the spring of 1996, the distance seemed to inject some hope into a marriage in which both had lost faith. Shawn had earned his pilot's license and was flying commercial jets for Jamaica Air. Among his benefits were free travel passes for himself and his family, affording them regular visits between Atlanta and Montego Bay. While many of the same familiar arguments—her refusal to consider moving back to Jamaica, and his expectation that she do the cooking and cleaning—crept into their visits, Shawn and Dionne lived and spoke as a couple in love, struggling to preserve a commuter marriage.

Commenting on Dionne's looks, the real estate developer says, "I would not say pretty, exactly, but a nice-looking woman, yes, a nice figure, a light complexion. In Jamaica, fair skin seems to be a plus. Every black man wants to marry a woman of lighter complexion. They feel it's a social uplifting. But I think it is a black thing, not a Jamaican thing. We call them brownings here. A man who wants a light-complexioned woman wants a browning."

Patricia Moreland, a stout-figured black woman in her early thirties with a pleasant round face and short-cropped hair, worked as an administrative coordinator at MARTA, during which time she hired Dionne Baugh as a secretary. On a rainy Sunday afternoon on Atlanta's south side, she explained to me that at MARTA she reported directly to an assistant general manager named Cheryl Carol. Moreland was looking for a savvy clerical assistant to help meet her boss's tough standards, which is how she came across Dionne. "Her demands, most times, were just so unrealistic,"

Moreland says of Carol. "And nobody could really talk to her. She was the only black female senior manager at MARTA, and there was a lot of pressure on her. She had a very strong personality. I was the only person she really wanted to deal with in our department, so when she fired her secretary, I had to go find her another one. That's when Dionne came in and applied.

"Dionne was this little fair, bright-skinned woman, and quite petite. And she had this little Jamaican accent thing goin' on. She wasn't really pretty to me. But the guys thought so because of her skin. You know, black men are really shallow when it comes to the complexion of women. So she looked very, very white, but she was not attractive to me at all. I mean, she was very petite and had a nice shape. She was the perfect thing for some politician or rich executive, you know, to show up at functions and just sit there. She had the long hair, and the mannerisms."

Patricia crosses her legs and puts her nose high in the air, giving her best rendition of haughty.

"It was like she was trained to be high class, like her parents sent her to etiquette school or something. She said all the right things during the interview. I told her about Cheryl, and how difficult she could be to work for, that until Cheryl felt comfortable around her, she probably wouldn't even bother talking to Dionne. I made it clear that I needed someone who would not feel threatened by that. That even though technically she worked for Cheryl, initially she would have to work through me until we could get Cheryl comfortable. Dionne was like"—Patricia's voice rises to a high, parodying pitch—" 'Oh, I'll just be here for you, to support whatever you need. There won't be any power issues. Whatever you say you need me for, I'll do it without any problems. I'm new to the city, and I'm just trying to get acclimated. All I want is to do my job.' So that was cool to me, and I hired her.

"I knew what Dionne was making. I still remember—she started off at twenty-one thousand dollars. That's not much money at all. But homegirl was dressed to the nines every day. From head to toe, she was sharp as a tack, like a thousand worth of clothes every day, and she never wore anything twice. You would have thought she was an executive. Over time, after I started to feel comfortable with her, I would say, 'Girl, what's up with you? Where do you get all the clothes?' And she would just smile. I mean, I started to feel like something wasn't quite right with her. I remember for Christmas she bought me this really expensive blouse. I still have it."

Patricia scurries off to her bedroom and returns with a red silk blouse, flecked with gold hues. "See," she says, handing me the blouse. "It's really nice. I was like, 'How did she afford this?' I mean, eight years later I still have it. It's gorgeous."

Dionne had lavish tastes, and Lance had begun to cater to them. Early in 1996, suspicions that Dionne was having an affair began to nag at Shawn, ignited by three disconcerting events. The first was Dionne's purchase of a nice four-bedroom house out in Norcross. Dionne had never told him that she was negotiating to buy property, but when he and Amanda arrived for a visit, she surprised them with it. She paid one hundred and eighty-nine thousand for the home, far more, he knew, than she could afford on her salary. But she explained this away as the product of many hard months of scrimping and saving.

Then came the Mercedes-Benz, which triggered a fight. Dionne had come to the airport to pick him and Amanda up in the expensive silver vehicle. He didn't want to start a shouting match in front of Amanda, so he waited until later that evening to question her about it. Sitting there in the kitchen—inside a house that to him remained inadequately accounted for—she spouted another half-baked, if not wholly false, explanation. A mentor, a successful entrepreneur who had taken an interest in her well-being, offered to sign for the car loan because of her poor credit, but she had made the down payment and was responsible for the monthly note.

"But we had gotten to be kind of like friends," Patricia says, taking the blouse back into the bedroom. She returns to her seat on the sofa. "Look, I just figured that because her father-in-law was some kind of ambassador in Jamaica, and with her husband being a pilot—or on his way to becoming a pilot, or something like that—she probably was set financially and really didn't even have to work. I would hear her on the phone sweet-talking her Shawn into sending more money for this or that.

"I knew she had men here in Atlanta. Somehow, I just knew it. She would say stuff like, 'I can get men to do anything I want them to do, so that's not really an issue.' And you know what? She wasn't lying. She had the men at MARTA wrapped around her finger. It became a kind of joke. Sometimes I'd test her, and say 'Dionne, go get such-and-such to do this,' and they'd do it. I was like, 'Okay, girl, go ahead and teach me somethin', because you are truly ballin'.'

"And she'd be like, 'I just know how to do it. I know how to work it.' I give it to her; Dionne had a way with men. Young white men, old white men, young black men, old black men. Any man. I don't know what she would say to them, but it worked.

"To be fair, she was doing very well at her job, too. She showed up every day on time, met all her deadlines, did whatever was needed. I was so happy. I'm like, 'Oh, Dionne, you just don't know how much pressure you're taking off me. Cheryl is comfortable with you, so now I'm able to step out and do more of the things I really need to be doing around here.' And that's when I made the mistake of letting my guard down.

"The longer Dionne was around, the more she tried to diminish my relationship with Cheryl. I'm not going to say that she wanted my job, but she wanted to have that direct connection to Cheryl. She started schmoozing Cheryl, and they were developing a good rapport, but still there were things in the office that Cheryl only discussed with me. Cheryl and I would have these confidential meetings in the conference room, and I would update her on things I felt she needed to know, and she would share things with me too that would help me in my work, mostly personnel issues. Dionne would be sitting at her desk outside the door, listening in on us. Information started leaking."

"What kind of information?"

Patricia Moreland sighs. "Okay, like Cheryl had a good friend named Donna, who worked at MARTA but maintained a friendship with Cheryl outside of the office. Everybody knew she was Cheryl's friend, so they didn't really mess with her. And Donna played on that because she knew folks were afraid of Cheryl. If she got caught not doing her job, she'd lie and say, 'Oh, Cheryl had me taking care of this or that,' and nobody would really question it. Well, in one of my meetings with Cheryl, I mentioned this to Cheryl, that Donna was using their personal relationship to avoid doing her job. So a couple of days after I said that, Donna's whole demeanor changed toward me. That kind of thing kept happening around the office, and gradually all my personal relationships just got really cold, but I still hadn't figured out why. It didn't really occur to me at the time that she was eavesdropping on my conversations, and using what she heard to destroy me.

"Also, I had some personal issues going on at home with my marriage. I met my husband when I was eleven years old, and we got married when I was twenty-one. I mean, the love of my life. I adored him, but I was losing him to drugs. In and out of rehab. It was the most difficult thing I've experienced in my life, to see my soul mate just deteriorate. Anyway, home was falling apart, and work followed. I was losing control of everything, but I didn't tell anyone what was going on except Cheryl. I went into an employee assistance program for a while, and after completing it I learned that Dionne had started this nasty rumor that I was breaking down because my husband was gay and had AIDS. This bitch was actually telling people to be careful about how they treated me because I was suffering through my husband's illness."

There is fury in Patricia's eyes now as she continues. "Dionne is evil. I confronted the bitch about it, and she could not deal with me. She just denied it, even though several people had told me what she was saying about me. I never got to the bottom of it, but I was so upset over everything, I left MARTA. It turned out that everyone in the department eventually quit because of Dionne. In the end, Cheryl was the only one left with Dionne. Of course it was too late, but Cheryl finally figured out that Dionne had run everyone out of there, and fired her. An executive in another department—a man, of course—hired Dionne as his secretary despite Cheryl's warnings not to. But I'll never forget, before I left MARTA, the last thing I did was walk up to Dionne and look her right in the eyes. 'You're vindictive and evil,' I said, 'and I don't know what you're trying to do, but it's going to catch up with you. You can't go around treating people like this. Everything you're doing to hurt people, it's all going to crumble around you one day. You'll see.' "

That process had already begun. The third and final sign that Dionne was cheating on Shawn came on August 6, 1996, the night before Lance's death, Shawn would later tell investigators. It was late, and Shawn and Dionne were in bed when the phone rang. He picked it up, and a man's voice asked, "May I speak with Dionne?" Shawn sat up, his temper rising. "Who is this?" he yelled, and the caller said, "This is Lance. May I speak to Dionne?" Shawn was furious. "Well, she's lying right here next to me," he replied. The man on the line said, "I thought you two were separated," and Shawn asked, "Is that what she told you?" The caller, getting impatient, said, "Look, just give her the phone." Shawn pressed, "Why do you need to speak with her?" He got no response except, "Man, just give her the phone. This is none of your business."

Shawn then asked the caller, "You planning on coming over here or something?" and the guy said, "That's right. Now put Dionne on." Shawn grudgingly handed the phone to Dionne, who never spoke to the caller, but simply hung up.

Shawn was furious—and a bit afraid. He asked Dionne who the hell that was. She told him it was just a good friend of hers, a nice guy who helps her with her schoolwork. Shawn asked whether this was the same guy who got the Mercedes for her, and she admitted that it was, which worried Shawn even more. He wondered whether the guy was dangerous, maybe a drug dealer who would come over and try to harm them physically. Dionne assured him that Lance wasn't a drug dealer.

Shawn's response that night was less than fierce; investigators called it wimpy. According to police transcripts, Shawn slept in a room above the garage that night, peeking outside every few minutes to see whether a strange car had driven up. The next morning, he packed his and Amanda's bags, and Dionne drove them to the airport. As he was departing, he told Dionne that she needed to figure out whether she wanted him, or whether she and this Lance guy were going to get together. Dionne assured him that she didn't want Lance; they had never slept together. Shawn insisted that she break off her relationship with Lance immediately, and that she return the Mercedes. She agreed, but she wanted to break things off gradually. Lance had been a good friend to her, and she didn't want to hurt him.

As Shawn and Amanda boarded the flight, he turned to look at Dionne. She waved, but her expression was strange—completely blank, as though she had gone to some other place, Shawn later recalled. He had never seen his wife look so distant. He was worried about her, and he told her earlier, no matter what she was feeling at that moment, not to go over to that man Lance's house that night. Dionne assured him that she would not. Whether in fact she did would later become the primary focus of the investigation. Baugh, maintaining her innocence, has always denied that she was at Lance's house that evening. Instead, she insists that Lance came by to visit her at her home on the evening of August 7, 1996, and brought his laptop for her to use.

chapter thirteen

THE INTERROGATION

Dionne sat down in the metal chair at the Roswell Police Department and glanced up at the lens hovering in the corner. The room was tiny; just the four white walls and three chairs. No windows. Not even a poster on the wall. Detective Anastasio pulled up a chair and took a hard look at this woman, Dionne Baugh.

Dionne exudes a calculated sensuality known to draw men to her. She stands five-foot-five in height and weighs one hundred and ten pounds. A head full of long black hair frames a smallish face with almond-shaped hazel eyes, a rather blunt nose, and full lips. Her complexion is almost alabaster. On many occasions, she has been mistaken for white. Her fair skin likely played a role in attracting Lance. Of course, he could have also been seduced by her manner, which comes across as coy and flirtatious. In her interview with Anastasio, she was playful, gazing at him with eyes that at moments were teasing and at others dismissive. Posed calmly in the chair, slender legs crossed and arms folded beneath a full bosom, she seemed almost to court Anastasio's approval.

Sporting jeans, a T-shirt, and a baseball cap, she began the meeting by implying she was underdressed for the cops' inquisition. She held up a hand to cover her face, protesting: "If I had known I was going on camera, I would look better."

"Oh, that's okay," Anastasio said. "You remember the last night you saw Lance?"

"Uh-huh."

"Try to remember what he had on."

Dionne's eyes, perhaps her most striking feature, searched the ceiling. "I want to say he was wearing a T-shirt, but I can't remember for sure," she said. "But most of the time he's always wearing a T-shirt and like greenish, grayish khaki pants. I don't remember specifically."

"Did the T-shirts that he wore have any labels on them, like a Braves T-shirt or Planet Hollywood or like that?"

"I think that sometimes he wears them plain and sometimes he wears them with different things on it," Dionne said. "I don't know. Everywhere he went he collected a T-shirt." She had a faint Jamaican accent.

"Oh, did he collect T-shirts?"

Dionne smiled. "Yeah, yeah," she said fondly. "Because I had gone to the Cayman Islands and I remember he called me and said, 'Don't forget my T-shirt,' and I said, 'You don't want anything else?' and he said, 'No, just a T-shirt.' "

Detective Edward Tucker stepped into the room and shut the door. He was considered among the more veteran interviewers at the department, so Anastasio had asked him to assist in questioning Baugh.

"When did you go to the Caymans?" Anastasio asked.

"When? Gosh, my memory has been so bad since this happened. Maybe two weeks before Lance died."

"Is it nice there?" Tucker asked.

"It's beautiful. It's wonderful, you should go," Dionne gushed. "Oh, and I was going to mention this to you. I'm glad we started talking about the islands. I'm going to Jamaica on Friday for a family reunion. Is there a problem with that?"

Anastasio looked at his partner and shrugged. "No, not at all," he said, even though he hoped to have her in custody by then. "I don't see a problem with it."

"I just thought I would mention it to you. I didn't want to leave and you be looking for me and think I skipped town or something. I didn't want to see my picture on TV over there on *America's Most Wanted*."

Anastasio found the *America's Most Wanted* remark to be strange, but skipped over it. "So you can't remember what he had on that night?"

"I don't," she said. "I really can't. I wish I could. I mean, I've gone over it in my mind so many times. I wish I had let him stay with me, I wish I had let him stay with me."

"Did he want to?" Anastasio asked.

"Yeah, but I don't know," she said, shaking her head regretfully, "I'd just dropped my daughter at the airport, and I was kind of depressed. I didn't want to be bothered with anybody. I just wanted to be there by myself, and he kept wanting to stay."

"What time did he come over to your house?"

"I don't remember the exact time. It was somewhere between nine and ten-thirty P.M., but I can't remember the exact time."

"Was it closer to nine, or was it closer to ten-thirty?" Tucker pressed. "Do you remember?"

"No, I can't remember," she said, waving off the question. "But let me ask you this. I saw his ex-wife on TV. Now, what's the progress of this investigation? Have you spoken with her?"

"Oh, absolutely," Anastasio said, and readied himself for Dionne to try to throw him off the trail. He knew it was coming, and was only vaguely disinterested in her sly finger-pointing.

"Okay, because I don't understand," she continued. "I mean, yes, that's his ex-wife. But she's still the mother of his son, and I can't understand how she's just all business, wants to take over the business. Lance wanted her away from that business so bad. I mean, every time we talked about her, it was, 'Jeannine has a great personality, but she's money hungry and she's a real bitch' when it comes to that. He never wanted her anywhere close to the business, so I can't understand why, you know, all of a sudden he's dead and she's appointed director for the business."

Anastasio nodded. "See, that's what I kind of want to talk to you about," he said, prodding her along. "Because there are some things that I just don't know, little things like that that Lance may have told you, like Jeannine has a great personality but he doesn't want her in the business."

"No, he wanted her as far away from the business as possible," Dionne rattled on. "As a matter of fact, we had a conversation one time, and he said, 'You know, if I ever win the lotto, I would sell'— there were these two companies who wanted his business, and he would sell it to one of them. And I said, 'Why don't you just save it, and maybe your son could inherit it one day.' And he just said, 'Hell, no. Jeannine could get it. No way.' "

"He didn't want her to get it?"

"No, and I just can't understand," she said. Her expression saddened, and then she asked, pouting, "Did you know that they had police there so I wasn't allowed to attend the funeral service, the ceremony?"

"Who had police there?" Anastasio asked.

"The mother," she said glumly. "There were two or three officers, and as I tried to walk in, he came over to me and said, Dionne, step aside. And I said, Who are you? How do you know me? And he said, We were hired by the family to make sure that you don't attend the service."

"Really?"

"I don't know. He just told me that I was not allowed to be there. And I asked him why, and he said he couldn't get into it, that it was the family's decision. I mean, what did they have against me? What have I done?"

"So how'd you meet Lance, anyway?" Anastasio asked.

Dionne Baugh was growing restless with Anastasio's questions. "At his birthday party." She sighed. "He invited my boss and me."

Anastasio knew this not to be true. In fact, Herndon had not actually invited Dionne but only her boss, according to Zonya Adams. Dionne, having opened the invitation and recognized Lance Herndon's name as a highly successful black computer consultant, phoned Access, told them that the invitation had been misplaced, and requested another. Upon receiving the replacement, she informed her boss that he had received two invitations, and asked him if she could go.

Anastasio decided not to call her on the lie. "So did Lance support you financially?" he asked.

Dionne blushed and looked sheepish. "Well, to a certain degree," she said. "He gave me money every week. He would pay for my school fee and buy my books. And he basically gave me a credit card, too, for whatever I needed."

"How much money did he give you a week?"

"It varied. Sometimes he would give me cash. Sometimes he would make a transfer at the bank, NationsBank, the one at the Lindbergh branch. He had a personal banker. I can't remember her name. He would call her, and she would do the transfer."

"How much money was it," Anastasio asked. "Fifties, hundreds?"

Dionne Baugh rolled her eyes and laughed.

"What can fifty dollars do? That's lunch money."

"To a police officer, that's a week's groceries," Tucker volleyed back. They all laughed.

"No, sometimes it would be seven hundred dollars, and sometimes it would be five hundred."

"Every week?"

Dionne nodded dismissively. "Basically," she said.

"Damn—nice guy."

Anastasio watched as Dionne's facial expression shifted from vanity to mock shame. "I'm so embarrassed." She giggled. "I hope it's not on camera."

"Don't be embarrassed," Tucker said.

"But, then again, I also helped him," she said. "I mean, I typed stuff for him."

"So you were being paid for services rendered," Tucker said, somewhat sarcastically.

"Those are your words. I won't add to it," she said. "I want to ask you, do you know or have you come across the name *Scott Kelly*?"

"No, ma'am," Anastasio said. He prepared himself for another trip down the blame game. He already knew that Kelly was Herndon's former attorney, who years ago had begun drawing up a will for Herndon, though the document was never completed.

"Okay, because he's supposed to be Lance's executor," Dionne said. "I'm not sure, but I remember a conversation Lance had. There was a painting that he wanted to give to a friend, and I can't remember exactly how the argument came up, but he said he wanted to give the oil painting to the friend, but the friend was gay. And I said, 'Well, how are you going to justify giving such an elaborate painting to a gay friend?' And he said, 'Oh, well, Mr. Kelly will make sure that he gets it.' And I was like, 'Well, why don't you make sure that your mom gives it to the person?' And he said, 'Are you crazy, my mom doesn't like anybody. I'll never leave her executor for my estate.' "

"Well, who is the executor of his estate?"

"I don't know. In the paper it says his mother. But it is so strange, as much as Lance was trying to fight people accusing him of being gay, that he would leave such an elaborate painting to a gay friend."

"Were people saying that he was gay?" Anastasio asked. He tried to look startled by this.

"Oh, his ex-wife accused him of it."

"She didn't say that to me," Anastasio said. "Do you know whether he was or not?"

Dionne screwed up her face. "I don't think he was," she said finally. "If I thought he was, I wouldn't have been with him. But he said his ex-wife often accused him of being gay. He said that she accused him of it, and that's why he didn't want to be with her anymore. I mean, the marriage had already gone bad when she started accusing him of that, and then it was, 'Oh, so you don't want to be with me because you're gay.' "

Anastasio decided to play along for a while. "Sometimes people do that as a defense mechanism," he added.

"He told me she accused him on more than one occasion. And he even said, 'Anytime you think that the gay mannerisms are starting to show up or something, let me know.' And I said, 'Well, I'll be looking for it.' But I didn't know what Jeannine was talking about, because I never saw that in Lance. But I realize that sometimes you're so close to somebody you really don't see what you should."

"Could the whole thing with women have anything to do with what he was going to a therapist about?" Anastasio asked.

"I can't tell you," Dionne said, but she was laying coy. Anastasio knew she was anxious to spill the beans. "I see that look on your face. He had me swear that if anything happened to him I would never reveal that to the public, because that was a private side of his life, and he never wanted anybody—"

"But you never know," Anastasio cut in. "I would hate for something that you're holding back in an attempt to be loyal to him become the key to why we don't get this solved."

"Well, he was molested as a child from the age of nine until maybe twelve," Dionne said.

"Male or female?" Anastasio asked.

"Male. And he had difficulty dealing with it, and said that's why he couldn't maintain a relationship because he always had urges to be with a man. He had never had any homosexual relationships, but he had urges."

"Oh, that's terrible. But you never knew him to be with a man?" Tucker asked.

"He told me he never did." Dionne's face was somber.

Tucker peered at Dionne, pulling his chair closer to her. "I'm going to ask you something personal. What kind of lover was he? Well, I mean, being a woman, can you say that you feel like there's no way somebody like him could be interested in a man? I mean, sometimes you can get a feel for that."

"Well, I encouraged him," Dionne said, sighing. "I said, 'If you really have the urges to be with a man, maybe you should try it one time and see if you like it.' He told me that's why he liked me so much, because at least with me he could be himself and never feel a need to put on a mask, but with everybody else he had to pretend to be something he really wasn't."

"Was he pretty straight when it came to sex, or was he into the kinky stuff?" Tucker asks. "I know it's hard, but we're just trying to get an idea . . ."

Dionne covered her face, laughing bashfully. "I don't know how to answer that," she said. "Oh, God, this is embarrassing."

"You understand it's necessary, of course, to ask this kind of stuff in this kind of investigation," Tucker said.

"He liked anal sex," Dionne said matter-of-factly.

"He liked anal sex? To the point of being obsessed with it?"

Dionne nodded. "And that's why I encouraged him to be with a man, because sometimes people are gay and they experiment with it and they, you know, adapt that lifestyle. . . . Please don't tell his mother that. She hates me."

"This is between us," Tucker lied. "I'm going to have to ask you something. Did he ever have anal sex with you? Did he try to push it on you? I mean, was he constantly hounding you about doing it and you wouldn't let him? Did he ever try to force it on you?"

"Uh-huh."

"To the point where you have to tell him, I'm out of here?"

"No, it never got to that point," she says.

"But he would try to force it?" Tucker prodded. "But he never succeeded? You were always able to stop him, or did he—I'm sorry, but I mean it's just things we have to ask."

Dionne looked at Tucker directly. "No, I engaged."

"Not because you wanted to, but because he forced you?"

"Well, *force* is a strong word," Dionne corrected. "Maybe I knew that's what he wanted and thought it would please him."

For more than two hours, Anastasio and Tucker pushed Dionne Baugh to recall the exact time Herndon visited her home, but she insisted she couldn't remember. She said Herndon stayed only five minutes or so, just long enough to drop off his credit card and the laptop computer and start an argument about Dionne's failure to have a home security system installed after he had already given her the money for it. Not in the mood for bickering, Dionne asked him to leave.

Late in the afternoon, unable to coax a confession from her, Detective Tucker decided it was time to come clean with their suspicions. "I'll tell you what I think," he said. "You know, this is Bill's case, his deal, but I'll tell you what I think. I think you went over there that night. I don't think he came to your house. And there's different things that prove that."

Dionne sat back in her chair and listened closely. "Uh-huh."

"Besides the surveillance system, there's other witnesses. So I think you went over there to his house on a pretext of returning the car to him or for some reason you thought you could work things out with him. You go there to be together. There's something that ticks you off. I think you got mad that he wasn't coming to court. You hit him over the head several times because you just flipped out."

"Like the fact that he had no intention of going to court with you that day," Anastasio said, a conclusion he drew after failing to find a court appointment on Lance's calendar.

"But I didn't know that," Dionne said, her voice still calm. "I didn't know he wasn't planning on coming."

"I think you got mad that he wasn't coming to court," Tucker continued. "You went back upstairs, you hit him over the head several times because you were just flipped out because you couldn't believe that he was doing this to you. At that time you took a laptop computer and you went home. And that's how I feel it happened. And I'm going to tell you now, any jury could understand something like that if someone was messing with them the way Lance played around on you."

The detectives also accused Dionne of calling a North Carolina furniture store and charging a three-thousand-dollar antique cabinet to Herndon's credit card the following day.

"You're wrong," Dionne said emphatically. "You're wrong. You're wrong."

"I think I'm right."

"Do I need to get an attorney?"

"That's entirely up to you," Tucker said.

"I mean, are you arresting me, or can I leave?"

"Well, you can leave, but there's one thing that we have to inform you of," Tucker said.

"What?"

"We have obtained a search warrant," Anastasio said.

"Okay."

"Which includes the car," Anastasio adds. "We're going to seize the car, and we're going to search your house."

"No problem," Dionne said, rising from her seat. "I just need to call my aunt to come give me a ride."

"Don't worry about it," Anastasio said. "Why don't you let us take you over there."

For the first time that afternoon, Dionne Baugh looked worried.

chapter fourteen

MOREHOUSE MAN

The Fulton County Courthouse, with its white Corinthian columns and high arched entrances, is a formidable structure. Looming in the shadow of the gold-domed Georgia State Capitol, the classically designed courthouse connects rather gracelessly to the county's government center, a postmodern building of slick steel and glass atriums. A neighbor to the Coca-Cola Company Museum and Atlanta Underground, a popular tourist attraction of subterranean boutiques and restaurants, this nine-story bureaucratic fortress occupies an entire square block of downtown Atlanta.

In the year that his friend Lance Herndon was killed, Paul Howard had risen to the building's highest office, becoming the

first black district attorney in Fulton County's history. A broadly
built man, Paul Howard is a forceful presence with a square dark
face and a bright, albeit infrequent, smile. Far more ambitious than
warm, Howard was born in the small south Georgia town of Mid-
vale, where he picked cotton and worked construction as a young
boy. His rise to local prominence was closely calculated, first by his
mother and later by himself. When he was a child, Howard's mother
had idolized the charismatic scholar and civil rights leader Dr. Ben-
jamin Mayes. Dr. Mayes had spoken before the congregation at her
church when she was a young girl growing up in Macon, Georgia,
and the experience left such a deep impression on her that Paul
would hear about it over and again during his childhood. "I wish
you could have seen that man," Howard recalls his mother telling
him. "He was the most handsome man I'd ever seen. I'll never
forget the sight of him standing at the podium wearing this white
suit, and this bright white shirt, and when he spoke, it was like he
was speaking from the heavens! His voice was so rich with intelli-
gence. When I found out that he had been educated at Morehouse
College, I said to myself right then that if I ever had a son, I'd want
him to go to Morehouse."

Although a top student in his 1968 high school graduating class,
Paul Howard applied to one college only—Morehouse. As Howard
began his freshman year that fall, the air on campus was still heavy
with anguish and anger over the April 1968 assassination of the col-
lege's greatest alumnus, Dr. Martin Luther King Jr. More than any
other accomplishment, Howard would cherish being a "Morehouse
Man," regarding the credential to be as impressive to blacks as Har-
vard is to whites. He went on to study law at Emory University and
upon graduation began rising through the ranks of the state law
system, as a tenacious Fulton County prosecutor and then as solici-
tor general, handling the county's misdemeanors.

In Howard's campaign for DA, Lance Herndon had served as a major contributor and raised thousands of dollars more, most recently hosting a big-ticket fundraiser at the home of the prominent attorney Ed Garland. He and Lance had developed a friendship during the campaign, which made solving his murder more than a professional matter.

One of Paul Howard's first initiatives as DA had been the formation of the Special Cases Division, an elite team of eight attorneys charged with prosecuting the county's most complex and high-profile homicides. While the team was comprised for the most part of veteran prosecutors, Howard made an exception for Clint Rucker, who, though only thirty-five years old, was probably the most naturally gifted trial attorney Howard had ever encountered. Howard's promotion of Clint aroused plenty of ire among Clint's more seasoned colleagues. There was much water-cooler grumbling that the newly minted black DA seemed to put most of his energy into nurturing the young black prosecutor as his "son" and handing him the best, most newsworthy cases.

In early April 1997, a few days after his disappointing meeting with Detective Anastasio and the Roswell police chief, Paul Howard called Clint into his office to vent his frustration over the Roswell PD's lack of evidence in the Lance Herndon case. With his young protégé sitting quietly across from him, Paul Howard told of how Lance had been his good friend for some time, a remarkably generous man who would have given anyone the shirt off his back.

"We need to put this case to rest," he told Clint. "Lance was killed back in August, and what we've got so far on this woman Dionne Baugh will never hold up in court."

Paul Howard grew thoughtful. Then he slid open his desk drawer. He took out a small clock and placed it on the desk. It was a simple timepiece set in a dark wooden frame.

"The last time I saw Lance, he gave this to me," Howard said. "It was a gift."

Clint looked confused.

"I know that you're thinking it's just a clock," Paul Howard went on to say. "But the thing about Lance was that he hated waiting on folks, couldn't stand people to show up late. He'd come over here and have to wait a few minutes because I was running behind on my meetings, and it always annoyed him when I wasn't on time. It became a kind of thing between us, with him saying I needed to get better control of my schedule. So this gift was his way of shaming me about my not respecting his time. It was a joke, but he was serious.

"My point is that Lance was a time freak, and a neat freak, too— you know, the kind of guy who ironed creases in his blue jeans. He always seemed to have it together, have things under control. You need to understand this about Lance, because I think that's how we're going to win this thing. That's how we're going to build this case. His obsession with time and certain other quirky patterns of his will help you build the evidence we need, even if it is only circumstantial. Lance was a peculiar dude, a highly organized, regimented, picky kind of brother. I need you to keep this in mind when you start talking to folks, and you'll be able to see your way through this. Trust me. If anybody can figure this out, it's you, Clint."

Over the next few weeks, Clint embarked on a crusade to fully understand Lance Herndon's habits, at work and socially. Lance's almost manic nature, his deft attention to detail, gradually began to crystallize into a profile of a man that Clint not only felt he understood but for whom he developed some empathy. Clint saw a bit of himself in Lance, especially in the Lone Ranger mys-

tique that seemed to inspire equal amounts of admiration and re-
sentment. Like Clint, Lance was self-made with New York roots
and had prevailed in his profession at a young age amid a chorus of
naysayers, opportunists, and sycophants. Lance, though, was cer-
tainly more organized than Clint. If opportunity always seemed to
fall into place naturally for Clint, Lance took nothing for granted.
The man was shrewd and resourceful, the sort who always looked
to make the best use of anyone around him. When Clint went to in-
terview Access employee Holly Steuber, she recounted to him how,
upon learning that she had studied art in college and possessed a
fine touch as a calligrapher, Lance put her in charge of his compa-
ny's Christmas card mailing.

"I'd sit home all November watching television and addressing
his many, many hundreds of Christmas cards," Steuber told Clint
in his office one afternoon. "He was very savvy at networking,
keeping his name in front of people, to the point that it was almost
funny. I mean, if he was talking to you and you were a sales lead
and you happened to mention that your son was graduating from
college next month, he'd make a note and then send a gift or some-
how acknowledge it in the next conversation. If your wife was
having a baby, he'd make sure to have a baby gift sent over. On sec-
retary's day he would send out Godiva chocolates to every secre-
tary working for a client or business associate.

"The man used to pride himself on leaving voice messages for
people. You know how a lot of people's voice mail has a date and
time stamp? So it would be like Sunday, five A.M. 'Hello, this is
Lance Herndon. I'm calling, etc.' Then people would call him back
and say, 'Man, you sure start early.' The people would think 'Wow,
that guy is something.' It was perception, and that's why he did it.
If somebody tried to blow him off and said call me in six months at
five o'clock, he'd call them in six months at five o'clock. He kept

meticulous notes on everything. He'd close his database every day. He was impossibly organized.

"For the Olympics he bought ten thousand dollars' worth of tickets and gave them out to friends and business associates. He *was* the business. It was his marketing, his PR, and his contacts with our customers and the people in the community. That's why he did things in the community, gave scholarships and charitable donations and things like that. The associations and business things that he did weren't really because he was so benevolent or philanthropic, it was because it was a means to an end. This is what a good businessman does. There's nothing wrong with that. It still means you do good things, but the motive wasn't to be a good person. The motive was to be a successful businessperson."

Lance Herndon was extremely fastidious, which Clint learned had led to some peculiar habits. Jackie told him that her son liked to take his power naps lying stiffly on his back, his arms folded over his chest, to avoid wrinkling his suits. He insisted on eating barbecue ribs with a knife and fork to keep his nail beds tidy. He showered and weighed himself a few times each day, kept weekly appointments with his barber and manicurist, insisted that Linda, his personal valet, prepare the exact same dishes each week, including his favorite of tuna salad, minus the mayonnaise. Toward the end, Lance could no longer afford to renew his contract with Linda, or his housekeeper Selma Joe for that matter. As time permitted, Lance had started cleaning his house and doing laundry himself. Still, the victim was not a man who lived by happenstance. As Paul Howard had suggested, a jury would need to understand and appreciate this above all else.

Clint also decided that a jury would need to view Dionne Baugh as pushy and manipulative. Selfish. Scorned. Lance's mother, Jackie, told Clint that she got a bad feeling in her gut upon meeting Dionne, and had warned Lance away from the woman. "I first came into contact with her last summer," Jackie told Clint. "She showed up at my house in Lance's Volvo and rang the bell, and as soon as I saw her, I said, 'Well, who are you? Do you work for Lance? Are you a friend of his?' And she said she came for Harrison's toys. There were toys that he played with at the park—you know, he had a truck and a tractor, a bucket, whatever—that I kept at my place because I would take him to the park now and then. Anyway, so I said, 'Well, you know, I don't just have anybody just show up at my door. I live by myself. People usually call me. My sister, anybody, they call me before they come to see me.' I didn't like that at all. I just felt like there's something not quite right with this woman, like she ought to know better than that.

"The other time I saw her, I was on my way into his house to work one day, and I saw Lance standing outside, and I could see she was in the Benz. I was making my way toward Lance just to say good morning. I could see her behind the windshield looking disheveled and crying or whatever. Then Lance just held his hand up like that, you know, indicating to me this was not a good time. So I just turned around and went on downstairs and went to work. Later on, I said to Lance, 'What's the problem? Why is she so upset? What's going on?' He said he'd tell me later, but I told him right then what I thought. I told him to be careful because she's a fatal attraction. I told him just like that, Clint. I sure did."

As he mulled what he was learning about the personalities of Lance and Dionne, Clint surmised that in Dionne's eyes, Lance was likely everything that her husband was not. While Lance thrived on amassing money and influence, Shawn was an unpretentious sort. He carried himself with the sort of humility that likely struck Dionne as too passive. If Lacey Banks was accurate in her assessment that Lance was on the brink of breaking things off with

Dionne on the night his body was found, some rage had likely been building in her. Dionne did not want to lose Lance, but was she capable of murder? An interview with Shawn revealed a woman with a hot temper that at times could become violent.

"Just the way she spoke to me wasn't normal," Shawn told Clint during the investigation. "I wasn't used to that, based on my family structure—her tones and insinuations. Basically, it was verbal abuse. She would speak down at me, and I wasn't used to that based on how I grew up, how my mom would speak to me. I kind of compared her to my relationship with my mom, and there was no comparison. I think that it was what affected our relationship the most. I never accepted the way she talked to me.

"She is very stubborn. If she makes up her mind about something, there's no way you can ever convince her of anything else. Like she's a Jehovah's Witness, and I'm a Christian, Anglican. So we have a conflict because I wanted her to come to church with me, and maybe that's being selfish because I don't want to go to the Kingdom Hall either. I want to bring our daughter into my religion, and Dionne objects to that. She speaks out against my religion, saying that we worship idols, and we're wicked people and her religion is the only way. It's not the things you say but how you say it, and she's not the type of person where you could sit down and have any form of dialogue and rectify any problem. She can be very disrespectful. Like going through customs, they might ask her to pay duty on an item, and she'd get real stink about it. She'd start looking down on them—I mean, the people are just doing their jobs.

"She's just not a very tolerant person. Like with Amanda, I think she's a good mother, but you see, she hasn't spent much time with Amanda. I've been like a mother and dad to Amanda, but Dionne has a very low tolerance with her. She doesn't just sit down and reason with her what's right from wrong from a mother to a daughter point of view. She would, you know, get real mad and even want to slap her if Amanda got out of place.

"Apart from our child, I think the one thing that's kept us together is our sex life. I mean, it is very good. But now that I've actually been threatening to divorce, she's very jealous. She thinks I have another woman, and that's the reason I want a divorce. She tried to break up my car in Jamaica. She's hit me across the face. She's grabbed my testicles so hard that I had to pry her fingers off. I've never seen this side of her, but the jealousy has gotten into her because she thinks I have somebody. Over the past six weeks of her being in Jamaica, for the whole month of December, I've been, you know, afraid of her.

"No, I haven't hit her in any way, but I have had to keep her off me. She broke into my room and took away all my travel documents, and made it look as if somebody had broken into my room from the outside. She told me to call the cops. She took my driver's license, social security card, and my residency, my proof of U.S. legal permanent residence. Now I have a hard time going through immigration. I reapplied for all that stuff, and it's going to be a hell of a long time before it will be replaced. She has them over at her house—she *told* me as much.

"If you're over there, man, could you please get my ID back for me? It's a pain in the ass—especially the green cards. I was really in love with Dionne. I still care for her, I guess, but I just don't know anymore."

On a cloudy Saturday morning in January 1998, Clint, dressed in his bathrobe and slippers, stepped out onto his front porch and picked up the *Atlanta Journal-Constitution* off the doormat. Making his way into the kitchen, he flipped to the front page of the local news section. The headline surprised him.

Arrest in Businessman's Slaying; Ex-Lover Charged in Bludgeoning:

Suspect's Divorce Trial Apparently Gave Cops Enough to Move in '96 Death of Roswell Entrepreneur, Lance Herndon

Earlier that week, Clint had spoken to Shawn Nelson's divorce attorney Michael Vogel, winning his support in using Shawn and Dionne's pending divorce trial to shed more light on her involvement with Lance Herndon. Her statements, Clint figured, might be used as leverage against her in the event she was charged with Herndon's murder. Without any real direct evidence connecting her to the crime, Clint was desperate for incriminating facts against Baugh. Nothing would have been more powerful than her own lies spoken under oath. Maybe she would have lied about knowing Herndon, or at least accepting money from him. But Paul Howard was too impatient. Fearing that Dionne was plotting to flee the country, which would have doomed the case and humiliated him in the process, Paul Howard had ordered her arrest before their case was airtight. Clint was livid.

evidence of a femme fatale

chapter fifteen

TWO ATLANTAS

The Honorable Jerry W. Baxter's smooth, glossy scalp adds an air of joviality to his longish face and sweet melancholy eyes. The quintessential southern gentleman, Judge Baxter has nothing crass about him; both his drawling speech and his civil manner are so deeply rooted that even his harshest words are tempered in folksy understatement. Sitting in his stately chambers at the Fulton County Superior Courthouse, Judge Baxter, a white man in his early sixties, is dressed nattily in a sky-blue seersucker suit, a rose-colored tie over a crisp white shirt, and white buck shoes, which are propped up on his big oak desk.

"Back when I was coming up, Atlanta's political system was always run by good ol' white boys," Judge Baxter tells me one warm spring morning in April 2002. "The county commission was just a gang of good ol' boys, and they ran things in the county with an iron fist. Not so much in the city, though. We had a pretty progressive mayor, Ivan Allen, back in the early sixties. And then there was a Jewish mayor, Sam Massell, who was a fine fellow and good with race relations. Then there was Maynard Jackson, our first black mayor. Once he took office, the political power gradually went to black Atlanta. These days, the sheriff and the DA and just about any political figure around here is black."

It is clear that Judge Baxter can't bring himself to speak Paul Howard's name. While not quite an adversary of the Fulton County DA, Baxter believes that Howard's hard-nosed, micromanaging approach at the office has the effect of not only slowing the judicial process but eroding morale in the DA's office, where an exodus of top legal talent has begun. The defectors have left a litany of complaints that Howard's bullying, second-guessing, and running their trials from the passenger's seat made working conditions unbearable to them.

Of course, Judge Baxter's view is colored partly by loyalty. His own star rose under Howard's fair-haired predecessor Lewis Slaton, whose connections ran deep in both white and black Atlanta. Slaten was simply a smoother politician than Howard, whose gruff manner runs opposite to that of the more amiable Slaten. While Paul Howard wins his battles with loud, heavy artillery, Slaten won his through a silent espionage of well-placed loyalists. Rarely missing the important funeral or wedding, Slaten reigned for nearly two decades as an old-style judicial kingpin, keeping the county's top legal matters scribbled on an envelope tucked in his breast pocket. Slaten's informal style became overwhelmed in the early 1980s by the popularity of crack cocaine and its attendant explosion of court cases. The end of his era opened the door for predominantly black Fulton County to elect its first African American into the office.

Just a few months before, Baxter had transferred from Fulton County's State Court, where he had presided for fifteen years, listening to folks bicker over money, car wrecks, and medical malpractice in civil suits. It was, in ways, a better living. Upon his arrival at Superior Court, his new colleagues toasted him with a party, then promptly rewarded him with their "dogs," handing over to him a fat backlog of the most ancient, tedious cases clogging the system. It was generally believed that such a backlog wouldn't have existed had Paul Howard not demanded that he review most of them personally, taking away the unfiltered discretion. In Baxter's view, the result has been, at last count, a personal docket saddled with more than three hundred criminal cases. He was slogging through them with yeomanly patience, all the while trying not to allow his mammoth workload to disrupt his sanity and optimism, which, at fifty-two years old, he refused to compromise.

In his own quiet way, Judge Baxter had other methods of rebelling against a justice system that turned well-meaning officials into hacks. One was his attire; frequently beneath his regal black robe, when weather permitted, he wore a pair of jogging shorts and white sneakers for a late-afternoon bicycling jaunt home. It was his way of not taking things too seriously. He recalled a time when a tenacious female prosecutor who passionately disagreed with his ruling came rushing up to the bench, ranting and raving at him. Baxter had but one reply for counsel: "Save it, lady. You're arguing with a man who doesn't even have his pants on."

Baxter runs a large hand across his scalp. "Atlanta has always been a fairly decent place, really," he continues. "We've had a few race riots, but they weren't really necessary. In any event, I think we've avoided a lot of real bad moments through leadership. Of course, when you leave Atlanta, out in some of the outlying areas, there's a feeling of hostility among whites who say Atlanta is run by blacks, and they've got all the money and they've got all the taxes and they've got this and that, so when they get in trouble, the hell with 'em. It's pretty bad out there. After all, this is still Georgia. There are people who are afraid to come downtown because they visualize crime and black menace coming down on them. You know, afraid of being robbed or whatever. Just petrified to come down here.

"The truth is, from my perspective, there's two Atlantas—a white Atlanta and a black Atlanta. Unfortunately, we're not fully integrated here. I mean, we work together and get along fairly well, but once everybody leaves their work, we pretty much go separate ways. Most of the wealthy black folks here in Atlanta live out in Cascade Heights. I live here in the city, in Midtown, where there's more integration. My children have grown up in fully integrated schools. They go to a public school where the ratio is probably seventy-thirty black. North Atlanta, where Lance lived, is where all the whites moved when they integrated the schools. The neighborhood here in the city where I grew up was just abandoned after they integrated the schools."

Baxter shakes his head in desperation. "It's crazy," he sighs. "That's why I try to get away whenever I can. I've got a little place in south Georgia. It's on the marsh on the river, just the most peaceful place. When I get through dealing with the murders and the rapes and the grandmothers and people crying and screaming, I just go down there and talk to the marsh people."

The judge closes his eyes and leans his head back. "I get down there, and oh my gosh, it's just all peace and quiet. I get down there as often as I can. I've got two weeks vacation coming up, and I can't wait. I've got an old boat I'm restoring." When Baxter opens his eyes, all the serenity has left his face. "I mean, some of the stuff I deal with, man," he says, shaking his head at me, "like the whole Lance Herndon thing, makes me feel horrible."

"I mean, it was just a little surprising, the number of women this fellow had and his lifestyle," Judge Baxter goes on, scratching his head. "I was taken aback by it all. The credit cards he let all the women have, and just the whole scenario. Maybe I've just led a sheltered life, or women have never sought after me like that. I've never had a lot of money, so maybe I can't relate, but this guy was something else. And I knew from the start this case was going to be trouble, because it was so old and there was so much confusion going on in his life."

On the morning of March 26, 2001, as the pretrial hearings began, Judge Baxter found himself gazing down from the bench and blinking his eyes hard. He was tired and a bit grumpy, having spent the previous night reading through the entire sordid transcript of Dionne Baugh's statement at the Roswell police station. He didn't dare express it to the attorneys standing before him, but he deeply resented the prospect of sitting through a five-year-old murder case—a case based purely on circumstantial evidence.

Even by the sluggish timetable on which justice typically is dispensed in Fulton County, this trial had taken a woefully long time in coming. To be sure, Paul Howard wasn't entirely to blame for the five-year lag between Herndon's death and Baugh going to trial. Herndon's body was found August 8, 1996, and within the first week, Anastasio and his investigators had their eye on Dionne Baugh as a primary suspect. Yet it wasn't until January 1998, or eighteen months later, that she was arrested, as the evidence against her hadn't been sufficient to seek an indictment. It was Howard's idea to have his own investigators watch Baugh during those eighteen months in case she somehow tripped up. His strategy worked: during her divorce proceedings against Shawn, she incriminated herself. According to those involved in the case, although on numerous occasions she had denied it to investigators, Dionne admitted to her mother-in-law that she had actually visited Herndon on the night of August 7, 1996.

The evidence against her, though, was still too thin to inspire much confidence in Howard, who may have acted in haste due to his gut fear that Dionne was planning to flee the country. Baugh's attorneys knew the state's case was weak, which is why soon after her arrest, they tried to talk her into plea-bargaining her charges down to involuntary manslaughter and seven years in prison. Swearing her innocence, she adamantly refused to negotiate. One of her attorneys, Michael Katz, recounted how Baugh was near hysteria her first days in prison. "She was like, 'Get me out of here!' " Katz recalls. "I mean, she's the kind of person who presents herself in a very classy way and likes wearing nice clothes. The last thing she wanted was to be wearing a county jail suit. That just wasn't her. She used to scream that she wanted her bottled water. She didn't want to spend a day in jail. She just didn't want to be there, period, even if she could have gotten one year."

Katz was retained after Baugh fired her first attorney for failing to get her released on bond. In the role of her new counsel, Katz succeeded in getting her out on a $150,000 bond, which her family promptly chipped in to pay the required 10 percent of. She took several weeks' leave from her job at MARTA, traveling quite a bit, to Montego Bay to spend time with her daughter, or relaxing in the Cayman Islands, her favorite getaway. She also took a few trips to Toronto to visit friends studying at the university there.

Further dampening Baxter's mood was the fact that Gerry Quinn had shown up in chambers that morning, announcing that he had joined the defense. Baugh's lead attorney, Michael Katz, in an apparent moment of self-doubt, had requested help from Quinn, a more seasoned trial attorney. Both Quinn and Katz were martial arts aficionados, their expertise being tae kwon do, and their restlessness that morning suggested that both men were eager to fight. The duo had, in fact, raised several legitimate pretrial points that Judge Baxter, despite his hopes for a swift proceeding, was forced to ponder.

Gerry Quinn told Judge Baxter that his most serious issue centered on Detective Anastasio's failure to read Dionne Baugh her Miranda rights during his aggressive and manipulative interrogation of her at the Roswell police station. Quinn insisted that his client's rights were violated, that the bullying atmosphere of the meeting made Baugh feel as though she was in custody when in fact she was not. That Anastasio obtained a search warrant for her automobile and house indicated that he viewed her as a primary suspect and focus of the investigation, and therefore he should have read her Miranda rights. "The detective did feel at the time that he had probable cause to arrest her," Quinn says. "The test is whether he was trying to find out general information or develop exculpatory information. And we think it was the latter. We think he deliberately delayed the reading of the Miranda until he had exhausted every form of trickery." Judge Baxter listened intently, even allowing Gerry Quinn to briefly question Anastasio on the stand, but in the end he ruled for the prosecution.

Also, in anticipation of the prosecution dredging up Baugh's trespassing arrest at Herndon's home, Quinn argued that the incident failed to accurately characterize his client's relationship to Herndon, a man simply covering up his affair with Kathi Collins, who was in his bed that evening. Why else, Quinn asked, would Herndon bail Baugh out of jail the following morning and continue an intimate relationship with her? Baxter rolled his eyes as Quinn continued. "Well, Lance should have brought the backpack down, thrown it out the door, and said, 'I will see you later,' is what he should have done. But, I mean, he calls the police out in acting—putting on a show for his girlfriend," the judge said.

Clint raised his hand to interject, but was outgunned by Gerry Quinn. "The key, Your Honor, is that Lance Herndon did not have her arrested," Quinn went on. "She spouted off to the Roswell police and said she wanted her books, and then she came back after they told her not to come back, and they made a unilateral decision to arrest her. Lance Herndon bails her out of jail and tells the other girl that he doesn't even know Dionne Baugh. The ultimate unreliability of all that, I mean, everything that man utters is untrue. Lance Herndon was so absolutely manipulative that it totally takes away any significance of the criminal trespass."

Again, Judge Baxter ruled with the state on the admissibility of the incident as evidence. "He called the police, and she was arrested outside his house. That's basically the bottom line," Baxter said. "So, what else have we got?"

Here, Clint deferred to his assistant counsel, Anna Green, a bookish blond whose case law background was superior to Clint's own. Green stepped toward the bench. "We just ask that the defendant not suggest someone other than the defendant murdered the victim—absent some basis in fact, some specific good-faith knowledge. I think the case law supports that. *Neal versus the State, Palmer versus the State.* Evidence which merely casts a bare suspicion upon another or simply creates an inference that another may have committed the crime is simply inadmissible, and we ask that any evidence or any reference or inference like that be excluded."

Baxter stroked his chin thoughtfully. "In this case, the way I understand it is that the victim is somebody with multiple relationships going on at the same time, and everything about his death is circumstantial. I mean, it is totally circumstantial."

"Your honor," Gerry Quinn cut in, "the cases that Ms. Green is citing, there is a confession, and there are fingerprints, and there is rock solid evidence that somebody did it. In those cases, the defense is that, 'Well, maybe the bushy-haired man did it instead.' But this case is not that: it is analogous to five people being in a lifeboat, everybody goes to sleep, and you wake up the next morning, and there is a knife in somebody's heart. It's one of the people in the lifeboat. Which one did it?"

Judge Baxter cleared his throat. "Look," he told Anna Green. "If you can't present me with a case where the facts are similar to the ones here, then I'm inclined to deny your motion. But if something comes up, and it's wild and crazy—and I can usually tell wild and crazy—then I will just rule on it." Baxter paused and peered at Gerry Quinn, who was holding a finger up to interject. "And you, Mr. Quinn, you are already getting wild and crazy, and you have got to cut it out."

"Sometimes I get that way," Quinn demurred. "I don't intend on doing that. Thank you, Judge."

Lastly, Quinn raised his concern that Herndon's high public profile against that of Baugh, an immigrant working as a secretary, might prejudice a jury.

"Judge, I know Mr. Rucker will use discretion in his opening statement," Quinn said, his voice dropping to a near whisper. "But I want to make sure that when we try this thing . . ." His words trailed off, and he started again. "What I mean is, apparently Mr. Herndon had won a lot of awards for being the black entrepreneur of the year and a bunch of things like that. I think it is fair to tell the jury that he was a successful businessman, but I don't want my client in the position of being charged with, you know, murdering Martin Luther King Jr. or something."

Rucker laughed sarcastically. "Sure, I'll agree not to go into his awards and the good things about his character if they agree not to trash his character."

"I can't agree to that," Quinn snapped back.

Judge Baxter rubbed his eyes in exhaustion. He had hoped that because both the victim and suspect were black, these proceedings might escape references to race, which always clouded everyone's thinking.

Born to devout Baptists, Baxter himself could hardly ponder the issue of race without recalling the harrowing experiences of his older brother Donald, who became a kind of racial guinea pig while studying at Mercer College, a Southern Baptist school located ninety miles south in Macon. Like most everything in the early 1960s, Mercer, while situated in the birthplace of such black talents as Otis Redding and Little Richard, stubbornly embraced segregationist admittance policies, a view reflected in their decidedly low-key attempt to finally integrate the school. Instead of recruiting a local Negro to attend Mercer, the college's Baptist missionaries traveled all the way to Ghana, hoping this English-educated West African might ruffle fewer feathers. Baxter's brother Donald, a star basketball player and aspiring preacher, agreed to accept the African as his roommate, but the campus rebellion was so strong—there were death threats, and obscenities and rocks hurled at the students—that even Dr. Martin Luther King Jr. and Ralph McGill, the famous liberal white editor of the *Atlanta-Constitution,* traveled down to Mercer and sat in the boys' dorm room to offer encouragement. Donald never broke under the pressure; and he and the Ghanain remained roommates until graduation, and still remain close friends. Baxter still admired his brother for that, and tried to keep his mind clear of racist thinking, which is why, unlike most folks he knew, he lived within city limits and sent his kids to a public school. And at the predominantly white Ainsley Golf Club, of which he was a longtime member, he counted among his best friends Milton Jones, an affable young black bank president and a real tiger on the back nine.

Judge Baxter brought his gavel down hard. "I'm going to let Mr. Rucker paint his client any way he wishes," he said. "Now, if there's nothing else, I'd like to move on."

When it was time to address the seventy potential jurors, Judge Baxter yawned heartily and expressed what he believed to be their collective sentiment. "Good grief, some of you are probably thinking," he said, "I'm down here, and really want to get out of this. I've got better things to do with my time."

Baxter assured them that the trial would not last beyond a week or so, and he reminded them that the time and wages lost are the sacrifice "all of us have to endure in order for us to live in a free and civilized society."

The crowd listened politely to Baxter's pronouncements before several hands flew up with all manner of excuses for dismissal. One man said he was undergoing radioactive iodine treatment; another's wife had just passed away, and he needed to stay home to care for his two-year-old daughter; a woman had just bought airline tickets to go home to Chicago for Easter; a DeKalb Tech student had exams coming up and couldn't afford to miss class; a worker for the American College of Nurse Midwives was scheduled to travel to Ethiopia; a man with diabetes held his chest, explaining sadly, "Judge, sometimes I be havin' seizures, and could pass out anywhere."

The heavy coverage of Lance Herndon's murder by local media resulted in Judge Baxter excusing several potential jurors during

voir dire due to their familiarity with the case. The judge also dis-
counted a man who said his Christian values prevented him from
keeping an open mind in a case fraught with "adultery and fornica-
tion." Two women who debated whether Dionne Baugh looked
more like pop singer Mariah Carey or the late Latin star Selena
were also passed over, while a male graduate student who, admit-
ting to having partied once at Lance's nightclub, The Vixen, proudly
gushed, "I had a great time with all the celebs hanging out there that
night," surprisingly found himself selected.

chapter sixteen

C-NOTES

As the trial began on a bright Monday morning in early April 2001, the showing in Judge Baxter's courtroom seemed to prove that Lance Herndon, once the man to know in town, had become the man people wanted to forget. His family had expected a strong show of support, a courtroom as packed as one of his parties; family, friends, clients, business associates, girlfriends, neighbors, flying buddies, and even a few curiosity seekers. Mostly, though, it was media; reporters whispering into cell phones and television camera crews jockeying for position. The investigation had turned up so much sleaze on Lance that even his closest friends stayed away for fear of sullying their own reputations.

Though not nearly as surprising, attendance for Dionne Baugh was meager, too, with only a couple of aunts and cousins having flown in from Kingston on her behalf. In the State of Georgia's bill of indictment, Dionne Baugh was charged with one count of aggravated assault and one count of felony murder in the death of Lance Herndon; two counts of theft for the illegal possession of Herndon's computer and credit card; and lastly, one count of financial transaction credit fraud for the unauthorized purchase of a three-thousand-dollar antique cabinet through the use of Herndon's Visa card after his death.

Flanked by her attorneys, Dionne Baugh was dressed like a corporate middle manager, in a navy blue pin-striped dress and black pumps. As Quinn and Katz shuffled papers back and forth, Dionne sat stoically between them, her fair skin paler than usual and her eyes sunken.

"The first time I saw her, she was sitting at the table with Quinn and Katz, and I thought she was an attorney," recalls juror Ben Wilson, a twenty-four-year-old computer software salesman at the time. "She was wearing a nice suit, her skirt just above her knees. She had nice legs. And she was very light-skinned—I thought she was Cuban or something. Anyway, when the judge said 'Will the accused please stand up?' and she stood, I was like 'Holy shit.' "

Clint waited patiently for the shifting and murmuring in the jury box to settle. "This," he began, "is the case of a greedy and controlling woman who targets a rich and powerful man. She seduces him with sex, and she attempts to control him throughout the relationship. And when those attempts are failing, the evidence will show that on August 8, 1996, Ms. Baugh was very angry. She confronted Mr. Herndon, and she killed him. That's really what this case is all about."

Clint looked over at Quinn, then back at the jury. "Who was Lance Herndon? He was forty-one years old at the time of his death. He stood five-ten and weighed about 150 pounds, and he originally hailed from New York City. He had been in the Atlanta area for about twenty years after a very prestigious academic career in undergrad. He moved to Atlanta with the hopes of starting his own company, and after a couple of years, that's exactly what he did. And the name of his company was Access Incorporated."

Quinn and Katz exchanged caustic glances, occasionally rolling their eyes as Clint spent the next couple of minutes describing Herndon's awards and accomplishments, from presidential recognition down to such impressive local achievements as setting up the latest 911 system for the city of Atlanta.

"You will hear Mr. Herndon described in a lot of ways," Clint said, his tone humble. "He was generous. He was fun-loving. He was almost anal about his cleanliness and organization. And one of the things you will hear is that with all the positive things going on in Mr. Herndon's life, there were also flaws, and primarily Mr. Herndon had two that you will hear about: he liked women, and he liked to spend money."

There were some arched eyebrows, blending into a soft chorus of groans and sighs in the jury box. Clint had anticipated as much, and continued matter-of-factly, "And it is within these two concepts—money and women—that he and the defendant connected, because, you see, Dionne Baugh liked to spend money—*Lance's money*. And if I were you, I would write down the letter C, just make a note of that letter, because we will come back to it during the course of this trial. You will find that Ms. Baugh received *cash*. She will tell you hundreds of dollars each week. A *car*, a 1996 Mercedes-Benz that she was allowed to use and was supposed to return. She received a *credit card* by which she could make authorized purchases. And from time to time, she was allowed to use his *computer,* an IBM laptop ThinkPad, to do some schoolwork."

For the next hour, Clint went on to paint Dionne Baugh as greedy and cunning, drawn to Herndon's generosity, yet in the end driven to murder him because of his attempts to break off their relationship, which had become the engine of her own lavish lifestyle.

It was a solid opening statement, made all the more impressive by the authority with which Clint delivered it. Judge Baxter sensed right away the jury's affection for Clint. "He's a salesman," Baxter would later tell me. "Any good lawyer has got to be a salesman. That's what it boils down to. You're selling your version of events. And he's likable and he's got the charisma sort of thing, too. He's a big guy, just sort of larger than life. It's just the way he smiles, and he flirts and struts around. And then he's wearing these really swank clothes. It all makes the jury like him, and they start believing in him."

As juror Ben Wilson gushed, "Clint Rucker was just awesome to watch. The women on the jury oohed and ahhed over him. It's true: the guy's a real badass, with the cuff links and three-hundred-dollar shoes and just a Hoss of a man, physically an imposing guy. And he seemed like a real good guy, too—someone who had all his ducks in a row."

Another juror, a middle-aged white woman named Sherrie Griggs, put it more simply. "If O. J. Simpson had been up against Clint Rucker instead of those other lawyers, he would be locked up today." Then Griggs paused, adding, "The problem was that he didn't have much evidence to work with at all."

It was Gerry Quinn who, in his opening statement, cast the first harsh light on the state's lack of evidence. He asked Dionne Baugh to rise, and the jury regarded her closely, doubtlessly noting her frailty. "The sole issue in this case is whether this man," Gerry Quinn said, pointing at Clint Rucker, "can prove beyond a reasonable doubt whether this hundred-pound woman made love to a man and, while he lay sleeping, smashed the life out of him. Can he prove that beyond a reasonable doubt?"

Quinn rested a hand on Dionne Baugh's shoulder, and she sat down. "As I listened to the opening statement, I heard a lot of noise," Quinn continued, "but I didn't hear much about real evidence. In other words, there was a lot of heat but not much light. Before this case is over, we're going to put you in the light business, folks.

"Lance Herndon was murdered five years ago, and for all those years, this woman has been laboring under these accusations, under these innuendoes, and to this day the state cannot tell you the time of death for Lance Herndon. They cannot tell you the murder weapon that killed Lance Herndon. They have no fingerprints of my client. They have no blood evidence related to my client. What they do have is a pubic hair, even though there's no question that my client and Lance Herndon were in a sexual relationship."

Gerry Quinn leaned in to the jury box. "Look," he said. "I don't mean any disrespect to Lance Herndon. He was a human being, and he did not deserve to be murdered, and there is no question that somebody murdered him. Mr. Rucker is correct that all of us have our good and bad points. But Lance Herndon, as the state has brought out, was sexually addicted. And to say that my client is a liar and a murderer? It could have just as easily been any one of his many women sitting here in court today, because if having sex with Lance Herndon is the equivalent of being his murderess, let me tell you, the list would grow mighty long."

The amused looks on many jurors' faces suggested that Quinn was slowly gaining their favor. A few even chuckled as he poked fun at the prosecution's assertion that Baugh, after sex with Herndon, bludgeoned him and began a Keystone kops–like scramble to find information and cover her tracks. He mimicked the notion of Baugh moving haphazardly back and forth across the mansion, checking his computer for his calendar, stealing jewelry off his dresser as well as his dead body, covering him with a comforter, and unplugging the telephone and alarm clocks—without leaving behind a single fingerprint.

"The state says my client had possession of Lance Herndon's computer," Quinn says. "But this time it didn't have a protective case, so therefore she must be a murderer. Folks, you will see this computer—it's somewhere in their bag of evidence. The thing is like a Sherman tank—it doesn't need a stinking bag, and even if it does, that doesn't prove anything! The issue is not whether there is a case on the computer. The issue is not whether she got a Mercedes-Benz, or whether she was going to have to give it up for a Ford. The issue is really not whether she had sex with Lance Herndon an hour or a day before he died, or whether she had sex at his house and lied about it or just met with him briefly at her house. The only issue here is whether this woman picked up a weapon and killed the man with it."

Taking the stand first was Lance's mother, Jackie Herndon, and it came as a relief to the defense that, at least on an emotional level, her testimony turned out to be rather unremarkable. Clint put Jackie, now sixty-four years old, on the stand as his opening witness, hoping to draw empathy from jurors; several of them were parents, and Clint hoped to use the grieving mother's horrifying recollection of finding her only child slaughtered to build some momentum with them. But at times Jackie Herndon came across more like a fond office colleague than an aggrieved mother, her words leavened by reason and sterilized by six years of prayer and acceptance. "When I went into the bedroom, my first thought was, 'Oh, God, this bed is not made up,' " she recalled. "It was all crumpled. It is a large king-size bed, and the comforter was all covered up, and the first thing I did was just instinctively pull the cover back; and that's when I found him there and his nose bleeding and his head all banged in, and that's just all I saw, you know, at that time. I screamed, hollered, called 911." Clint asked her to identify several items, including a pair of purple shorts, a gray novelty New York City T-shirt, a pair of white sneakers, each of which she was wearing as she flailed about the scene that morning, as well as a bath towel she had draped over Lance's head. But Clint's efforts to spark Jackie Herndon's emotions by showing her these bloodstained articles failed. And the courtroom audience, whose eyes, at least initially, had tried to bore through Jackie's brittle facade, finally drifted away back into themselves, shifting it seemed to their own matters outside the courtroom.

"No further questions."

Juror Sherrie Griggs is the wife of a retired top executive for Home Depot and the mother of two sons, ages sixteen and seventeen. Her background, she says, helped her empathize with the women in Lance Herndon's life, particularly Jackie Herndon, who somehow survived finding her son beaten to death. "I sat right up in the front row, closest to Clint Rucker," Griggs says late one night from her home in Florida, where she and her family now live. "I had never been on jury duty in my life, so the whole experience was just a lot for me to take in. It was so depressing. I mean, just really depressing going in there every day listening to how this man was murdered, and looking at the autopsy photos and the murder scene."

Clint couldn't help feeling slightly discouraged as he ceded the floor to the defense. From the outset, Jackie Herndon had told Clint she doubted his ability to successfully prosecute this case. In their first meeting nearly four years ago, she quizzed him on how long he had been with the DA's office, how many murder cases he had prosecuted, and of those, how many he had won, and it was clear by Jackie's expression that she believed that the state had assigned her case to a rookie who was in over his head. As Rucker sat down, Jackie watched him for a moment and then averted her eyes.

In the chess match of trial law, attorneys are always careful to place themselves opposite the right witness on the stand, and in this case the defense decided that Gerry Quinn's aggressive style of examination was best aimed at those least likely to inspire sympathy among jurors; Michael Katz was more suited for the soft-touch questioning, such as with Jackie Herndon and ex-wife Jeannine, who by then had remarried and moved with Harrison, now ten years old, back to Kansas City, as well as with those others not expected to yield breakthroughs for Baugh's case. But Katz's performance proved more fruitful than anticipated, as Jackie Herndon soberly reviewed her son's financial affairs, which, she discovered after his death, were in shambles.

"It was your understanding that at one time Access was a multimillion-dollar company?" Katz asked.

"I don't get into millions," Jackie said. "You know, it was doing well."

"And so you don't have any idea how it came to be that there was no money?"

"Oh, no, no."

Indeed, the week that Lance was murdered should have been a pay week for Access employees. The first one to realize the company was broke was Zonya Adams. She had signing privileges on his Fidelity brokerage account, and when she went by a branch to make a withdrawal to pay some of Access's outstanding debts, she was informed that the account was twelve dollars overdrawn. She and Jeannine called one of Lance's contacts at NationsBank, explained their cash problem, and asked whether they could sell their receivables to the bank. But the banker, after expressing his sympathy and saying how much he admired Lance and his business, told Jeannine that Lance already had an outstanding $125,000 credit line that was past due and needed to be settled immediately.

The following week, one of Lance's contractors filed a lawsuit, demanding several thousand dollars in back pay. Jackie Herndon protested, furnishing receipts for checks she had written and given to Lance to pay. But over the next few days, it became clear that Lance had never mailed out those checks. They found them tucked away in the office. Meanwhile, the bills were piling up, and so were the threats. Jackie Herndon sold the Volvo, for which Lance had paid cash, for twenty-eight thousand dollars just to keep employees at bay, but news kept getting worse. Jackie had no choice but to let Holly Steuber go—she couldn't afford to pay her. Zonya, bless her heart, agreed to work without pay.

As it turned out, Lance owed about fifty thousand dollars to contractors, and another seventy-five thousand or so to credit card companies. Along with his house, Lance owned three rental properties, only one of which had a tenant. Without any income, Jackie was forced to sell all three properties dirt cheap. Two months later, unable to pay the huge mortgage on Lance's main residence, she was forced to sell it at a bargain-basement price.

Lance had also stopped paying his taxes. Beneath a stack of papers in his office desk drawer was a 1994 tax return, prepared and signed by his accountant, but Lance had never mailed it in. His lapse in paying the IRS was particularly depressing because it suggested Lance had been in bad financial shape for quite some time, longer than any of them had imagined. Somehow he had managed to keep his woes hidden. Still, it was almost eerily coincidental to Zonya and Jeannine that Lance was murdered on the very day that Access wouldn't have met payroll.

This would have been a first for Access—in all its years operating, Lance had never once missed meeting payroll. It was crazy thinking, but at one point the women thought maybe, just maybe, Lance wasn't dead at all and had actually faked his death and fled to some foreign country to avoid the shame of financial ruin. For a moment, though not long, they actually wondered whether Lance might be in South America somewhere. He loved South America. That is where he'd likely go. Admittedly, it was wishful thinking. But when they mentioned this theory to Jacques, he quickly set them straight. He had seen the body at the morgue. He wished they were right, but the dead man was definitely Lance.

The question of who would take the reins of Access also became a contentious, slippery issue, moving from such candidates as Zonya (not experienced enough) to an outside consultant (too expensive) before ending up in Jeannine's hands. But the succession was short-lived. At one point, Jeannine and Zonya had set up a meeting with Fulton County, one of Lance's longtime clients, hoping to renew some of the contracts that had recently expired. Jackie, not wanting to be cut out of the loop, decided she should go along as well. The trio made an odd-looking bunch, with Jeannine and Zonya dressed up in their business suits and pumps and Jackie extra casual in a straw hat with a scarf tied around it and a sundress. Not long after the women sat down, the Fulton County official politely explained, his eyes seemingly fixed on Jackie, "I'm sorry, but we won't be able to renew your contract because we're moving away from doing business with mom-and-pop shops." A few days later, Access shut its doors for good.

The revelation of Lance's financial crises stunned the jury. They watched while Jackie Herndon recalled how, as executor of her son's estate she had been left to resolve a quagmire of unsettled business and personal accounts. With his bank credit lines pushed to their limits, Jackie Herndon was not only unable to meet the firm's payroll but faced restive contractors and creditors who threatened litigation. By her estimate, Herndon owed in excess of half a million dollars to various parties. "We did not take any money," she testified. "I did not pay myself. Zonya did not take any money, either. We could not pay staff because we didn't have anything to pay with. So in lieu of that, we paid off the contractors. Kept them happy. We were willing to work without."

When Katz posed the question, "Did it surprise you that he died without a will?" one of the jurors gasped audibly. As the exchange played itself out, Rucker's body tensed visibly, as though he was ready to leap from his seat to object to the question's relevance, but instead he sat quietly through Jackie Herndon's sheepish response— an attack he should have prepared her for.

"I guess I never really thought of it in those terms," she replied. "I don't think I was surprised because he probably didn't think he was going to die so young, you know what I mean. If he were eighty years old or something like that, and in ill health, I would think he would have a will. But being healthy and vibrant and so concerned about his health and everything, dying was probably the last thing on his mind."

As one of Lance's former employees would later tell me, "There were odd things that would come up, checks that would bounce. He did make good on them, but one of the things he used to do was switch money around all the time. So I don't know if there were errors when he moved money around, or if he truly had a cash-flow problem. It's hard to know because he was so sneaky.

"The thing is that during the last couple of years, the business was not at its peak, but he still spent money the same way he always had. His heart wasn't in it anymore. He was really getting into the music business and wanting to do all this other stuff. Access was making money, but he spent too much, and what ultimately ended up happening was, he went through his reserves.

"I remember one time," the employee continued, "there was a payroll problem of some sort, and Lance had somebody write up a letter. The language was atrocious, but it was on Fidelity Investments letterhead. That's where he kept his brokerage account and wrote his checks from." The employee kept a copy of the letter, which appears to be a bootleg explanation and apology from Fidelity for mismanaging Herndon's account, signed by a company vice president.

"Lance used to do stuff like that. He'd make it up if he thought he could get out of trouble. Here's something else. He had the Porsche. He had the Jag. And he had a Volvo he was really trying to sell just before he was killed. He used to drive that Volvo all the time because he didn't want to rack up the miles on his other cars. But he disconnected the Volvo's odometer so the mileage wouldn't rack up. But this is how tidy he was: he had printed out on sticky notes the different RPMs, and he would stick them on the dashboard so he would know how fast he was going. The sticky notes would say something like 3,000 RPMs equals 50 miles per hour and so on. Every once in a while he'd hook it back up and then unhook it. I think the car showed something like 85,000 miles when he was trying to sell it, but it really had something like 150,000 miles on it."

———

Through Jackie Herndon's testimony, though it was only peripheral to the larger question of Baugh's guilt, the defense had succeeded in setting in motion a gradual tainting of Herndon's image. If Clint had triumphed in his opening statement by painting Lance as a polished, worldly entrepreneur, the defense had now brought him down several notches. With Lance portrayed as a shadowy figure whose grand reputation as a businessman was built atop a sinking foundation, it would be easier to cast doubt on the reliability of other witness testimony.

Instead of trying to restore the luster to Lance's bruised image, Clint homed in on his unerring sense of routine, his obsession with time and organization, and his fastidious hygiene. The jury looked weary as they listened to Clint, who began pressing his way through the tedium of a timeline of who, on the day and evening prior to Herndon's death, had seen his IBM laptop computer, whether it was or wasn't enclosed in its protective covering, Herndon's views regarding loaning the computer to nonemployees, and various other work habits that revealed a strong sense of his routine.

Jeannine Herndon, radiant in a black sleeveless dress, aroused some intrigue, or at least wanton stares from the men scattered about the courtroom, when she took the stand. Even Judge Baxter seemed momentarily more attentive as he listened to Jeannine's soft-spoken testimony. She was undaunted by Katz's personal questions about her ex-husband's infidelity, and her testimony had the overall effect of advancing Clint's theme of Lance's strict and unwavering work regimen.

Both Zonya Adams and Holly Steuber, in their turn on the stand, proved sure-footed, though hardly riveting witnesses. Both clearly remembered the laptop's condition and whereabouts when they left the Access office at 6:00 P.M. "It was on my desk," Zonya Adams said. Clint was initially encouraged by the resolute manner in which his witnesses were able to specifically place this key bit of evidence at Lance's home on the night of his murder—that is, until he glanced over and observed a group of jurors yawning in full chorus.

Juror Sherrie Griggs said that while she took copious notes of the timeline, others were starting to get bored. "There was this one black gal who sat two seats away from me," she recalled. "She kept falling asleep. It was really bad because everybody could see her. We would pat her on the back and give her candy, anything to keep her awake. It was awful."

A few minutes later, during Katz's cross-examination of these witnesses, Gerry Quinn himself spotted the slumbering juror, a young black woman with long braids, her eyes closed and head nodding back and forth. During a brief recess, Quinn approached the bench and alerted Judge Baxter that one of the jurors was snoozing. "That could be a problem," Baxter replied, his own eyes glazed over. "If we catch 'em nodding off again, maybe we'll have to get them some coffee. Heck, I could use a cup myself."

Clint's simple goal was to depict a fastidious, organized man who kept a tight rein on his belongings. He needed to establish this character trait to prove that Dionne was lying about not being at Lance's home on the night of his death. He could place her there in two ways: Dionne had told her mother-in-law she went to Lance's, and she was in possession of an item confirmed to have still been at Lance's home by those who last saw him alive. Clint planned to set these facts before the jury in his closing argument.

The jolt for everyone came when Lacey Banks, eight months pregnant and dressed dowdily in a blue maternity blouse and slacks, underwent Quinn's cross-examination. She had breezed through

Clint's questioning, but Quinn was eager to unveil her longtime affair with Herndon and exploit the fact the she was the last to see him alive. Quinn looked somewhat disarmed by the newlywed soccer mom sitting before him. Still, he pushed forward, unwilling to allow her newfound family values to derail his strategy of casting her as one of Lance's unscrupulous mistresses.

"Now, you used to have a sexual relationship with Lance, correct?"

"Correct."

"And how long ago did that start?"

"I knew Lance for maybe twelve years. I would say probably after the first year."

"All right. Did you continue to have sex with him after he got married?"

Clint Rucker jumped from his seat furious. "Objection, Your Honor," he shouted. "Relevance."

"Your Honor, sexual relationships between the parties in a case can point to bias and motive," Quinn said calmly.

Judge Baxter nodded. "I overrule the objection."

"So the truth is that you and Lance had a sexual relationship when he was married to Jeannine, correct?"

"Yes."

"And the truth is, the reason the marriage broke up, among other things, is that she found a naked picture of you, isn't that correct?"

"No, I don't think so," Lacey said.

"Did you ever tell the police that you used to have sex with Lance, and Kathi's picture would be on the bed stand, and you and Lance would turn it down?"

"I don't know that I said that."

"Did you do that?"

"Yes."

"And sometimes you and Lance, knowing that Kathi was the girlfriend, would put the photograph facedown, and you would laugh?"

"I wouldn't say we would laugh. It wasn't a laughing matter. It was just something that was a ritual for him."

"Excuse me?"

"I said it wasn't a laughing matter. It was a ritual for him."

"A ritual for him that whenever he would have sex with you, he would put Kathi's picture down?"

"That's not just with me."

"Oh, with the other women as well?"

"Correct."

"Isn't it a fact that the last time you had sex with Lance before he died was the Wednesday before?"

"I have no—I don't know."

"But that could have been the case, correct?"

"Well, we had tapered off our relationship on that aspect. So I don't know."

"But you, nevertheless, were still having sex with Lance close to the time that he was killed?"

"That's possible."

"But he called you that night and asked you to marry him, didn't he?"

"It wasn't like that. He said you should consider that. That was a joke with us. It wasn't like he was proposing to me, no."

"So, you left Lance Herndon's at ten thirty-seven that night? And how long did you say it takes you to get home?"

"That night it was kind of foggy. I would say twenty, maybe thirty minutes."

"According to the statement you gave the police officer, when you arrived home at eleven twenty-nine, the answering-machine message from Lance was already there."

"That's possible."

"Forty-some-odd minutes? Could it take that long in the fog?"

"I don't remember. I don't think it would have taken that long."

"This card, Exhibit Seven, with your handwriting. Who was it sent to?"

"A girl by the name of Rachel."

"Rachel Morris?"

"I don't remember her last name."

"But this is your handwriting, correct? Not Lance's."

"Correct."

"Did Lance sign it?"

"Lance signed it, yes."

"How did that make you feel?"

"It didn't bother me at all."

"Even though you just had sex with him the Wednesday before?"

"That's not what our relationship was about."

"Even though he called you that very same night and asked you to marry him?"

"That was always a standing joke. Again, it was not a proposal."

"Now, at the time Lance died, you had a boyfriend, correct?"

"Yes."

"What was that boyfriend's name?"

"Jimmy Turner."

"Did he have a nickname, Sweet?"

"Yes."

"And did Sweet know that you and Lance were having sex just as friends?"

"No."

"Is that something you kept from Sweet?"

"At that point in our relationship, between he and I—it was irrelevant."

"Irrelevant to you, or irrelevant to Sweet?"

"To Sweet."

"No further questions."

Next on the stand was Kathi Collins, who seemed to relish this very public moment. Quinn watched eagerly as she answered Clint's questions with wry humor and aplomb, entertaining jurors with wistful recollections of life as Herndon's companion on the high-powered circuit in which he worked and socialized. "Yes, we attended several business awards presentations, as well as music awards shows in Los Angeles. We went to the mayor's parties, entrepreneurial business breakfasts and dinners, a variety of functions," Kathi Collins waxed. But her sanguine demeanor quickly turned catty under Gerry Quinn's cross-examination. Like Lacey, Kathi was married by now—in fact, Hayden Eastman, her alibi on the night Lance was killed, was now her husband. Quinn pressed hard to portray Collins as among several plausible suspects overlooked by Roswell police in their haste to charge his client.

"Would it be true that at the time you started dating Lance, you were married and Lance was married? Is that correct?"

"Yes."

"Would it be true that Lance was concerned that a private detective might be following you?"

"Yes."

"Is it true that you tried to hide your relationship because of the private detective that Lance was afraid his wife had hired?"

"No, there was no issue. He thought private detectives might be following him, but we still went out. We weren't intimate at that time."

"Okay, that was back in '93, but certainly by January of 1996, you had started to date Lance Herndon on an intimate basis, correct?"

"Yes."

"And somehow almost every stitch of clothes you owned got over to Lance's house?"

Kathi smiled. "Not nearly *every* stitch."

"So you had a lot more clothes than this jury has heard about?"

Kathi tossed her hair and nodded emphatically. "Yes, a *lot* more."

The jury burst out in laughter. It was here, Quinn later admitted, that he knew he was losing this witness and the jury. Kathi was plastic and self-absorbed, but nothing more. "It's like none of these people had a soul," Quinn said later of those in Lance Herndon's circle. "They were just having sex with anybody. And so here she is, Miss Hollywood, and I'm thinking she would just self-destruct up there. I mean, the jury couldn't stand her. They hated her. But I don't think we were able to establish her as a likely candidate for murder."

As juror Ben Wilson recalled, "I didn't like Kathi Collins one bit. She was the most arrogant person I'd ever seen, just this real stuck-up person. I couldn't believe she got up there with that kind of attitude. But on the other hand, I could definitely see how a guy could be attracted to her. She may have been annoying, but she was absolutely beautiful. A really pretty face, long hair, and slim but muscular body—like a middle-distance runner or something."

As Quinn pushed on, Kathi seemed to relish the attention, smiling and smirking and flirting through his questions. "Didn't you tell the police that of all the girls, Lance loved you the most?"

"I said that I thought Lance liked me best because he dated several women while he was separated from his wife," she said, matter-of-factly. "But when he got his divorce, he asked to date me again. So, yes."

"Did you have any idea that Lance was having a sexual relationship with Lacey Banks?"

"No, I didn't."

"Did you have any idea that Lance was having a relationship with Dionne?"

"No."

"Did he tell you he had been making love to her for several months? Did he tell you that?"

"No."

"Did he tell you that he bought her a Mercedes?"

"No."

"Were you surprised when you found that out?"

"I believe he gave her a Mercedes," Kathi said, rolling her eyes, "which is a *leased* vehicle in the name of Access Incorporated. Is Dionne's name on the Mercedes?"

"How did it make you feel that she was driving the Mercedes?"

"Indifferent, because I don't think you can own a *leased* vehicle that belongs to the bank."

"So that's what makes the difference, not who drives it? It's whose name is on the lease?" Quinn said. But his tone was deflated. "No further questions."

During the seven-day trial, some twenty-five witnesses took the stand, several of whom were forensics and medical specialists from the Georgia Bureau of Investigation brought in by the prosecution to discuss physical evidence linking Baugh to the crime scene. Special agent Sam House, guided by large maps and photographs set up on easels, reviewed his team's processing of the crime scene. His briefing focused largely on clarifying a range of demonstrative visual evidence put before the jury, such as blood spatter and smears on the wall, bloodstained sheets, gum wrappers found in the driveway, head and pubic hair samples, fingerprints, and carpet footprint traces.

The most critical aspect of this presentation, though, was not the grisly photographs themselves but what several jurors perceived as Dionne's nonchalance when faced with the images projected on the screen. "A lot of us couldn't bear the sight of those pictures," Griggs said. "They were horrible. I looked at them for a second and then turned away. And then I looked at Dionne. The same pictures were on the screen of her attorney's laptop, and her face was two inches from that screen, looking directly at it. Even her family had gotten up and left the courtroom because they didn't want to see those pictures. But Dionne didn't have any problem looking at them. It was like she was mesmerized by what she was seeing."

Following Sam House, forensic serologist and DNA analyst Keith Goff testified that on or beneath three of ten fingernail clippings taken from the victim, the DNA of someone other than Herndon was found. He said that when the samples of the unknown DNA were analyzed, the profile matched Dionne Baugh. Clint used Goff's testimony to further buttress his assertion that Herndon's obsession with hygiene made it likely that Baugh's skin found beneath Herndon's fingernails was fresh—not days old. This was a point he had worked to establish earlier through Jackie Herndon, who had described how her son enjoyed eating barbecued ribs with a knife and fork.

Keith Goff also added that swabbings of the victim's penis revealed the presence of amylase, an enzyme found in its highest concentrations in saliva. The DNA in the amylase was consistent with Lance's. Clint used this statement to strongly suggest that upon kissing Lance, this amylase was transferred from Dionne's tongue to Lance's penis during oral sex, a hypothesis Goff did not refute.

But in Katz's cross-examination of forensics and DNA experts, he neutralized Clint's headway by raising the possibility that the matching head and pubic hair discovered on Lance could have resulted from contact with Baugh days before his death, while marveling over the Georgia Bureau of Investigation's inability to match hair evidence found on the scene to anyone interviewed by Roswell police. The state's DNA evidence, Katz argued, was equally weak, as experts could not reliably cite the length of time Dionne's skin had been beneath Lance's fingernails.

Clint's witness, a middle-aged black woman named Selma Joe, drew a dubious reaction from the jury with her tale of a potential murder weapon. Selma Joe was the owner of Joe's Janitorial Service, whom Lance once contracted for the biweekly cleaning, dusting, and vacuuming of his residence. She testified about the abrupt appearance of a large crescent wrench Lance had found in his home, and said that he pointedly questioned her about it, saying he had not purchased it himself and was therefore curious about its origins. "I had told police about it," Selma Joe told Clint. "I had asked them what did they think Mr. Herndon had been killed with, and at the time, they said they didn't know. And I believe at that time I told them that there was a wrench in the house that Mr. Herndon was concerned with because he called me."

She went on to recount that she had described the object to Clint, and that he sent out an investigator to take her to Home Depot and identify a wrench similar to the one Lance found at his home. This store-bought wrench, about a foot long and seven pounds, was entered in evidence as State Exhibit 45. Yet the spectacle played poorly to the jury. When Clint placed the wrench in Selma Joe's hand, she herself looked unconvinced. "This one has a point on the end. The one we saw was more round than this. Plus, this one isn't long enough. The one at Mr. Herndon's was longer." There were frowns in the jury box as Selma Joe handed the mock murder weapon back over to Clint.

Katz exploited the weakness in Selma Joe's testimony. In his cross-examination, he pummeled the possibility that the state had a plausible murder weapon, pointing out that Selma Joe's employment under Herndon began in September of 1995 and ended in December 1995, eight months before his death.

"During all those months after you stopped working for Mr. Herndon, you didn't know where that wrench was, or who had that wrench, correct?"

"Correct."

"So it is fair to say that to this day, eight months after you last worked there, were in his residence, he is killed, and we don't know where that wrench went, do we?"

"No."

"You don't know if he moved it between the last time you saw or talked to him, and when he was killed, do you?"

"No."

"You just know that you didn't see it anymore—eight months before he was dead?"

"I know I didn't see it when I came back to clean his house after he was killed."

"You mean, eight months later?"

"Yes."

"No further questions."

Perhaps the most damaging testimony to Dionne came from her own cousin Dawnette Angela Lounds, an attractive, fair-skinned young sports agent whose recollections of past conversations with Dionne added credence to Clint's portrayal of the defendant as a scorned gold digger.

The petite Lounds was already weeping when she took the stand. At Rucker's prompting, she explained that she and Dionne were first cousins, their mothers being sisters, and that their blood relationship gave them a natural closeness. But she said Lance had also played a significant role in her life, first as a lover and later as a mentor who helped her to build her own sports marketing firm. As a result, Lounds testified, she was upset when Dionne, days after being introduced to Lance at his forty-first birthday party, called her to inquire about his financial status and whether he spent his money generously on the women he dated.

Her voice quivering, Lounds said that she told Dionne that Lance wasn't the kind of man who simply doled out cash on a casual basis. Lounds also recounted that, days after Lance's death, Dionne had phoned her and made light of his murder, chuckling as she wondered whether his death was possibly drug-related or the work of his ex-wife Jeannine. "I told her that any involvement with drugs wouldn't be like Lance, and Jeannine wasn't capable of doing anything like that." Her last conversation with Dionne, she said, occurred during her aunt's funeral. "At the funeral we went aside, and Dionne said that blood is thicker than water. Why was I siding with Jeannine? And I told Dionne that I'm not siding with anyone. I haven't spoken to anyone but the detective, and whoever did it will have to pay the penalty," Lounds said.

This could have been a knockout blow for Dionne's character, but at each turn, the defense was able to exploit the many weaknesses in Lounds's testimony, as with most of the other evidence and testimony put before them. Gerry Quinn dredged up, for instance, Lound's bitter confrontation with Shawn, who apparently

accused Dawnette of steering Dionne away from him toward At-
lanta Hawks basketball players. "And that altercation got so heated
that Dionne had to step in between you two, didn't she?"

"Yes."

"And that was related to Shawn's jealousy of Dionne, wasn't it?"

"Yes."

"In fact, Shawn was accusing you of being a bad influence on
her, correct?"

"It was about me taking her to the Hawks game."

"And supposedly going out for possibly meeting or seeing men,
correct? Isn't that what he was upset about?"

"Right."

"He was upset enough that you and him almost got into
fisticuffs?"

"Yes."

"Would you say that over the period of time you had known
Shawn, he had a pretty jealous streak in him?"

"Yes," Lounds says, her eyes wandering to Clint, who sat
glumly as his star witness slipped away.

But it was Detective Anastasio's police work that took the harsh-
est blows during the trial. In his questioning, Clint tried to
guide Anastasio through a smooth, seamless testimony, but Quinn
made this difficult by pointing out that several of the conclusions
drawn by Anastasio's statements were based on hearsay rather than
fact. "Were you able to determine whether or not the body had
been moved prior to the arrival of any police officers?" Clint asked
Anastasio at one point.

"It was my understanding from speaking to the supervisor on
the scene."

"Your Honor, again, this is hearsay," Quinn objected, exasperated by Rucker's missteps.

In another instance, while examining Anastasio about his August 9 interview with Kathi Collins, Rucker asked, "Was she cooperative?"

"Yes, she was," Anastasio replied.

"Did you have a chance to interview her regarding her whereabouts on the previous evening?"

"Yes, I did."

"And did you take her at face value?"

"No. Ms. Collins was able to provide verification that she had been on a flight attending a funeral and had landed in the Birmingham area on a flight, I believe, with her niece. She had that information. Plus she was able to provide a gas receipt from a gas station somewhere between Alabama and Atlanta. She arrived back in Atlanta on the night of the seventh and went to a restaurant called Embers in Sandy Springs."

Jumping to his feet, Quinn objected vehemently. "All of this is hearsay!" he said. "And another thing I want to object to, the prosecution will ask, 'Did you take hair from this lady, and wasn't she cooperative?' But he fails to say whether or not Dionne Baugh was cooperative."

The "hearsay rule" prohibits attorneys from arguing a case through secondhand testimony, requiring instead the sworn statement of actual eyewitnesses. The rationale here is that without the eyewitness on hand, the opposition lacks the ability to cross-examine. In this case, Clint should have questioned Kathi or another witness regarding her whereabouts rather than putting the question to Detective Anastasio. He also should not have prodded the detective into bolstering the credibility of other witnesses as a way of casting doubt on Dionne's innocence.

The court sustained several of Quinn's objections regarding hearsay. And later, during his exhaustive cross-examination of Anastasio, he made the Roswell detective squirm and stammer as he forced him to defend both the thoroughness and the integrity of his investigation. Anastasio's face turned ashen as Quinn blitzed him on each angle of a probe he characterized as sloppy, misguided, and at times built on questionable ethics.

"My client told you about seven times during your interview with her that she couldn't be sure exactly what time Lance Herndon came to her house, didn't she?"

"Seven times? I don't know how many times she may have said that."

"But she said it a lot, didn't she?"

"Yeah."

"Then you guys told her a bunch of lies, didn't you? You told her there was a video that caught her on tape, and there was no video, was there?"

"No, there wasn't."

"And you and your partner, Detective Skip Tucker, told her that you had a palm print of her. You actually said that, that her print was on the nightstand."

"He said we have a palm print, and whose he said it was I don't remember."

"And so you are accusing my client of doing some lying in this interview, but are you are going to fess up that you were lying to her?"

"Oh, I was."

"And Skip was lying to her?"

"Yes, he was."

"Didn't she ask you if it was necessary to go into all these details of Lance's sex life? Didn't she express reluctance because

Lance's family might have to hear all these detail of their sex life, didn't she?"

"Correct."

"And you told her the family wouldn't have to be exposed to that, didn't you, even though you knew that the videotape of that interview would be used as evidence?"

"At that point I did not, because she wasn't arrested."

"But she expressed concern about Mr. Herndon's family having to know the details of his sex life, right?"

"Correct."

"So let me ask you, Detective, is there any limit to the number of lies a police officer can tell in such an interview?"

"There is not a guideline. It is a judgmental, subjective, case-by-case issue, person by person."

"So in the course of a police investigation, at least during the interview of the suspect, there is an unlimited, carte blanche ability of the officer to lie?"

"If you need to."

"Okay. And you just keep lying and lying and lying until you get to the truth as you expect the truth is," Quinn said, his expression bewildered. "Did you know that Lacey Banks's boyfriend had borrowed some money from Herndon?"

"Yes. Jimmy Sweet Turner."

"Right, and he's got a criminal record, too, doesn't he?"

"From what I understand, yeah."

"Did you interview Sweet Turner?"

"No, not personally. I'm not sure if one of the other investigators did. I did not."

"Okay. Well, I'm a little curious, because you've got a man dead. You've got a boyfriend that owes the dead man money, with a car seen in the neighborhood about the time of the murder, and he has got a criminal record, and he was never interviewed?"

"Well, I didn't know at the time if Mr. Turner had previously owed Mr. Herndon or currently owed money. I thought it was previous. And based on the way the investigation was going, panning out on this end, we took it that way."

Gerry Quinn pressed Anastasio hard on his decision not to look further into Turner—to probe his phone record or compare shoe impressions found at the scene to Turner's footprint. "We weren't sure that the footprints on the back steps were relevant to the crime scene, since the crime scene was in the house and contained in the master bedroom," Anastasio said in defense. "They were photocopied and videotaped. So they were documented. But we don't know—we don't know whose footprints they are."

"And to this day, you don't know?"

"No, we don't."

The grilling of Anastasio continued throughout the afternoon, as long expressions fell across the faces of the members of the jury. Rucker, too, sat pensively in his seat as favor seemed to drift further away from him. Now and then he mumbled into the ear of assistant attorneys Anna Green and Phyllis Clerk, who could scarcely camouflage their own looks of defeat.

Meanwhile, Dionne Baugh leaned back in her seat and for a moment allowed herself the brief luxury of an expression, the corners of her tight lips curling slightly upward in a manner that seemed to approach satisfaction.

chapter seventeen

"ABANDONED AND MALIGNANT HEART"

Clint Rucker watched quietly as Gerry Quinn stepped over to address the jury. Quinn's eyes were weary, his expression solemn. It had been a long week for all, Quinn told them, but the time spent examining this case was worth every second because the outcome would affect his client Dionne Baugh every day for the rest of her life.

"This is the most important job you will ever have," he said. "You literally have the fate of a fellow human being in your hands."

A few in the jury box had been slumping, but when he said this, they eased up straighter in their seats. They were, after all, being entrusted with a decision of terribly great consequence. Judge Baxter's platitudes about duty and democracy and all the handbook stuff about juries being "the people's last safeguard against unjust law and tyranny" had congealed into something more than abstraction. Staring at them now was a question that seemed grotesquely out of proportion to all the imperfect souls among them elected to answer it. It was this irony, perhaps more than anything else, that made this moment feel so frightening, humbling, and ennobling at once.

They looked exhausted, too, but Quinn was seasoned at touching the raw nerves of his audience, a veteran at mining and then tugging at those hidden heartstrings that connected them to his message. With his slow southern drawl slightly hoarse from the past six grueling days, Quinn stood before them and shook his head earnestly.

"Thank goodness for America," he said. "In America, it doesn't matter if you like Dionne Baugh. In America, it doesn't matter that Lance Herndon was a well-respected person who died, and that you feel sympathy. Because I feel sympathy. Especially for the mom. Especially for the wonderful wife. What a wonderful person she is. How he ever got sidetracked, I will never know. But in America, no matter how important socially the victim was, every criminal defendant has a right to be judged under the law. The law says that the state has the burden to prove the case beyond a reasonable doubt. And in this case, the state has failed to meet that burden."

He paused, his jaw tightening. He paced the floor for a moment before stepping back to the jury. "The state has to prove that she killed him. Not that she lied or was mistaken about the phone calls and whether Lance was molested and all the silly stuff they made time charts on. The state has to put a dagger through her heart by showing that she killed somebody. Where is the evidence that she killed someone? Where is the evidence that she was even mad at Lance? The state doesn't even have to show motive, but I would like to know what her motive was? What the state has done is spend six days of our lives trashing Dionne Baugh, and not really address-ing the issue. Is there any eyewitness in this case that will say she was there? No. Is there any eyewitness saying that she hurt some-body? No. Is there any person to tell you she was mad at Lance Herndon? No. Is there a murder weapon? No. Is there one iota of evidence that she got blood on her? No."

Quinn peered at Clint. "This lady has rights, and they sat here and virtually crucified her with innuendo," he said. "Don't let innu-endo, and don't let a loud powerful voice by an extremely skilled prosecutor substitute for evidence."

It was a fierce attack, and over the next ninety minutes the jury sat mesmerized as Quinn turned the state's case into his own per-sonal piñata, bashing and poking holes in it from every conceivable angle. Quinn was theatrical in his parody of the investigation and sparked laughter when he mused, "For five years, they sat around and did nothing with the case until they were forced to try it, and then they start scrambling around for a murder weapon. They went on a shopping spree. They go pick up a tire tool, then a baseball bat, and they discard each weapon until, finally, they come up with this hokey wrench that's bought at the store. This really is America—if you can't find a murder weapon, then you go out and buy one!"

Quinn made impassioned appeals to the jury's sense of reason and logic, arguing that even the hardest physical evidence brought by the prosecution had failed to validate the charge of murder. "The DNA under his fingernails. Was that incriminating? Not really. If you have sex with someone, the DNA will stay under the fingernails for days, and what the expert witness said was that it was not just going to wash out in one washing. It is going to wash out eventually. But let's just say the very worst. Let's just say the very worst is that she lied about having sex with him. She lied about her coming over because she was scared to put herself at a murder scene. I'm not saying that happened, but let's just give the state that—that she really did have sex with him that night. What does that prove? She made love to Lance, and then she left. So what? Mere presence at the scene of a crime is not enough to convict. I will say it again. Mere presence at the scene of a crime is not enough to convict."

Clint glanced over at Jackie Herndon, who sat somberly at the rear of the courtroom. He felt panic rising in him. Jackie Herndon had predicted how this trial would turn out, how her son's name would get dragged through the mud, how detective Anastasio's case—based on flimsy circumstantial evidence and hearsay—would get picked apart and ridiculed by any defense attorney with even an ounce of skill. Now Rucker feared that a conviction was fading from him fast, that the jurors whose faces seemed to soften with each of Quinn's final words would rule for an acquittal. "My client is in your hands," Quinn said solemnly. "Thank you, and God bless you."

The courtroom was quiet. Clint rose from his seat. He wasn't ready to face the jury. Instead, he reached down and picked up a glass jar sitting on the table. He had borrowed the jar from his mother's kitchen cabinet the previous afternoon, filling it with sand and water from the creek running behind her home in Decatur. The jar cradled in his massive hands, Clint's gaze drifted out into the courtroom and looked at each member of Lance Herndon's family, variously crestfallen in expression. And then Clint's eyes fell on his own mother, Carolyn, who offered him an affirmative nod. Walking slowly toward the jury box, Rucker began to speak in a soft, deliberate tone.

"We've spent about six days presenting you with a great deal of evidence," Clint said. "A lot of facts, a lot of circumstances. In listening to Mr. Quinn's closing argument, I am reminded of a story by the author Victor Hugo. Mr. Hugo tells a story about an octopus. You see, the octopus has trouble defending itself. It does not have a beak like a bird, or claws like a mountain lion to ward off its attackers. Instead, what an octopus has to defend itself is an ink bag. When an octopus feels threatened or gets scared, what the octopus does is release some ink into the water. And by doing that he clouds the water, makes it dark and murky so that you can't see through it. That's how the octopus escapes.

"That's what Mr. Quinn has been doing to you, muddying up the water so you can't see clearly. So before I go on, I'm going to show you something. It is just a mason jar filled with a little creek water and some sand at the bottom. I brought it here today to illustrate a point, and the point is this: the state's case is clear, as clear as the water in this jar now. But watch this."

Clint shook the glass jar hard and held it up above his head. "You see what happened to that clear water," he said. "Yes, it's all cloudy now. You can't see through it anymore." Clint stepped over and placed the jar, in which the brown sand was now swirling, on the edge of the jury box. "Okay," he continued. "I'm going to talk about the facts of this case for a while, and if you keep your minds focused, I can promise you this—by the time I'm finished talking, the truth about who killed Lance Herndon will become crystal clear to you. And so will the water in this jar."

His hands clasped thoughtfully beneath his chin, Clint stepped away from the jury and paced the floor for a moment. "Now, I want to talk to you about the evidence of the defendant's guilt," he said. "The evidence in this case proves that Dionne Baugh was at Lance Herndon's house at the same time that he was killed. The evidence proves that Dionne Baugh avoided the police, that she lied about her whereabouts during the time that Herndon was killed. The evidence proves that Dionne Baugh is the killer through DNA, blood spatter, and hair. The evidence proves that Dionne Baugh was in possession of items that were taken from Lance Herndon's house by the killer.

"The judge is going to tell you that in a murder case, the state does not have to prove motive. I don't have to show a reason for the killing, and I guess that's a pretty good law because murder is bad enough in and of itself. A defendant doesn't get to have a good reason why they killed—all I have to do is prove that they did it, because there really is no good reason to commit a murder. But in this case, we all know what the motive is. It is greed. Greed! And I wanted to make sure, so I looked it up. Covetousness, possessiveness, meanness, hoarding, insatiable, graspingness, envy, spite. See also jealousy. All those words describe this defendant.

"And let me tell you what the book says is the opposite of greed. It is generosity. Who does that sound like in this case? Sounds like Lance Herndon. Here is a man who gave this defendant, this greedy defendant, his own credit card so that she could take her own family out to dinner, whom he had never met. That's who Lance Herndon was. He was a man who just wanted to make everybody happy. Here was a man who even though he was suffering financially continued to reach out to all the other people around him and help pull them up. Do you think it is a coincidence that so many people can be involved with this man in a very intimate way, and then come into court and speak so fondly? But see, when this greedy and controlling woman met this rich and powerful man, she must have figured she had hit the jackpot. But when he would not go along with her foolishness, she killed him. She killed him."

As Clint spoke, the events of that night, back on August 7, 1996, which had perplexed him for some time, fell into place. He would later recall that: in his mind's eye he saw Dionne Baugh standing there, looking at Lance before stepping into the bathroom of his master suite.

*L*ance had showered and was undressed and sitting up in bed, watching an erotic video, when Dionne returned to the bedroom, still fully clothed. He wanted her to join him in bed, but she was reluctant. She was distracted, her mind on the problems Lance had caused her. By tomorrow's court appearance on trespassing charges. By Lance's ill-timed call to her home last night and the argument it had caused with her husband. By the funky attitude Lacey had when Dionne called earlier that night to speak with Lance.

Dionne stepped over to Lance. She told him she was worried about the trespassing charge, and Lance assured her that he planned to appear to get the charges dropped, to explain to the judge that the incident was a misunderstanding. He eased Dionne toward him, but again she resisted. She sat quietly on the edge of the bed as Lance watched porn play out on the television screen.

*M*opping sweat from his brow, Clint paused and painstakingly explained the charges to the jury. Dionne Baugh was guilty of what is technically referred to as both "express and implied malice murder," meaning there was a deliberate intention to take away the life of another human being, despite a lack of considerable provocation by the victim. "All the circumstances of the killing show an abandoned and malignant heart," he said. "He didn't provoke her. And let's look at the way she killed him, because the manner of death proves that Dionne Baugh intended to kill him." Clint was still there inside the bedroom at 9060 Bluffview Trace. He imagined it all.

A few moments later, Dionne rose from the bed and unbuttoned her blouse. She let her skirt pool at her feet, and she slid into bed beside Lance. Sex had never been a problem between them. Dionne felt that she understood Lance, his many fetishes and fantasies. But there was something unsettling about him tonight, about her place in this scene of heavy purring and groaning and the slapping of flesh on the television screen. She felt cheap, like one of those porn actresses that Lance used for foreplay. Lying beside her, his head propped up on a pillow, Lance seemed like a stranger to her now.

Clint's mind was churning now, and his heart was pumping so furiously that he felt dehydrated. As he reached down to take a sip of ice water, he saw his cocounsel Phyllis Clerk offering him a nod of encouragement. A surge of adrenaline went through him. "It is funny how defense attorneys like to make light of circumstantial evidence," he continued. "They want to convince you that somehow it's not as good as direct evidence. But I have seen eyewitnesses come into the courtroom and lie and change their story. The thing with circumstantial evidence is that it doesn't lie." Rucker stepped over to the jury, his eyes connecting with each one of them. "You may not realize it," he says, "but you use circumstantial evidence every single day of your life. You make life decisions based on it."

By the end of his life, Lance Herndon was struggling in his both his business and personally. His once-successful company was losing money and his attempt to break into Atlanta's thriving entertainment industry as an artist manager had failed. (*Courtesy of Fulton County District Attorneys Office*)

Lance's relationship with Kathi Collins began to unravel a few months before his death. Police discovered this photograph tucked behind the framed photograph in his bedroom. *(Courtesy of Fulton County District Attorneys Office)*

Investigators also speculated that one of Lacey's boyfriends may have discovered her affair with Lance and murdered him in jealousy. (*Courtesy of Lacey Banks*)

Lance became part owner of a popular Atlanta nightclub called The Vixen. He hoped the venture would be an entreé into the entertainment business. (*Courtesy of Holly Steuber*)

Calendar

	Start	End	Category	Description
	9:00 PM	11:55 PM		THE HONORABLE ANDREW YOUNG, SUSAN J. ROSS, MICHAEL LANGFORD & LEON SAUNDERS INVITE YOU TO KARAMU / THE AFRICAN OLYMPIC HOUSE 98 CURRIER ST (1 BLOCK NORTH OF RALPH MCGILL) LIVE ENTERTAINMENT: BEAL RT & NATIONAL JAZZ TRUMPETER, MELVIN MILLER & 'BOUT TYME FEATURING VOCALIST, BARBRIA DE'ANNE OPEN BAR, CULINARY DELIGHTS, LIVE DISC JOCKEY INVITATION ONLY; RSVP 404-261-1378 (LM ON VM 7/23(
4	6:00 AM	6:00 AM	Personal, Travel, Vacation	MAYBE J. HARRISON TO FL.
5	6:00 AM	6:00 AM	Travel, Vacation, Personal	GRANDMA AUSTIN IS INTOWN FORM 8/6TILL 8/26
	6:45 PM	7:45 PM	Meetings, People, Projects	LINDA WORKS
6	5:30 AM	5:30 AM		DO YOU WANT TO RUN EMPL AD ON SUNDAY?
	10:00 AM	12:15 PM		ADELE AUSTIN / DELTA FLT 611 LVS NYC 10AM ARVS ATL 12:13PM
	12:00 PM	1:00 PM		MEEGAN PAYNE / CTY OF ATL OFFC OF CONTRACT COMPLIANCE 404-330-6992 ROUNDTABLE DISCUSSION
	1:30 PM	2:30 PM	Projects, Meetings, Issues	MEET WITH STACY—LHH'Z'
	10:50 AM	12:20 PM		ELVER HERNDON / DELTA FLT 1229 LVS RICHMOND 10:50AM ARVS ATL 12:19PM
	12:00 PM	1:00 PM		TAKE 993 IN...
	6:15 PM	6:15 PM	Issues, Meetings, Projects	WORKING
	7:00 PM	8:00 PM		TENTATIVE: TED RUBENSTEIN TO SEE THE VOLVO H–404-377-7183; W–404-827-2853
8				
9	6:00 AM	6:00 AM		KATHI WORKING THE APPAREL MART
	9:00 AM	10:00 AM		VERTiS MCMANUS / SPECTRONICS CORP. 770-455-9750 CONF CALL... SETUP MEETING WITH MARC...!!!
	5:00 PM	7:00 PM	People, Personal, Projects	WORKOUT...
10	12:00 PM	12:00 PM		KING HISTORIC DISTRICT NATIONAL PARK SVC VISITOR'S CTR 450 AUBURN AVE FREE ADMISSION, OPEN 7 DAYS 8-6 THRU 6/23 OPEN 8-11 AFTER 6/23 404-331-5190
11	6:00 AM	7:00 AM		KATHI WORKING THE APPAREL MART
	12:00 PM	1:00 PM		WORKOUT...
	3:00 PM	4:00 PM		TONY DOZIER & FELICIA @MICK'S PARK PLACE ACROSS FROM PERIMETER MALL 404-696-8500; POR-404-235-8614
12	6:00 AM	6:00 AM	Travel, Vacation, Personal	GRANDMA AUSTIN IS INTOWN FORM 8/6TILL 8/26

STATE'S EXHIBIT 19

Throughout his career, Lance was known for maintaining a tedious personal calendar, which listed appointments as far as two years into the future. On the morning Lance's body was discovered, his staff noted the calendar entry field for that day was curiously blank. (*Courtesy of Fulton County District Attorneys Office*)

Dionne Baugh, a naturalized Jamaican immigrant, began dating Lance shortly after meeting him at his forty-first birthday party. Lance courted the married Georgia State University student with cash and gifts, which included this Mercedes Benz. (*Courtesy of Fulton County District Attorneys Office*)

24
1 4
21 month

AGREEMENT

This is a formal written agreement between Lance Herndon & Dionne Baugh for a Mercedes C220. Both parties agree to the conditions binding this agreement.

Lance will pay for the car commencing July 1996 and not to exceed July 1998. Dionne will take over the payments as soon as she can, but will not surpass August 1998, at which time all paperwork including but not limited to the title of the car will transfer in Dionne's name.

until 21 months from 1st month payment

I Dionne agrees to surrender the car if I decide to leave the relationship before July 1998. I Lance promises not to force or do anything that will cause Dionne to exit the relationship without reasons of her own.

I Lance agrees to give Dionne ample time to secure some other means of transportation (approximately 2 months) if I terminate the relationship.

We both realize that we live in a world that is plagued with obstacles and imperfections. Therefore, relationships come to an end due to irreconcilable differences. If this occurs, Lance has the authority to made the final decision on what happens with the car. He has the option to sell the car to recover his money or he may give it to his mother. The choice is his. Nevertheless, if Dionne endures the relationship until July 1998 the car is her, she has the right to do whatever she wants. However, if she seeks to trade in the car before July 1998, she can do so only at Lance's discretion.

It our relationship escalate to the point of engagement or marriage, this agreement is null and void.

_____   _____   _____   _____
Lance Herndon   Date   Dionne Baugh   Date

Upon seizing the Mercedes Benz from Dionne Baugh, police discovered a pair of unsigned letters in the glove compartment. The documents, typed by Baugh, sought to give her legal ownership of the vehicle in the event of Lance's death or a split in their relationship. (*Courtesy of Fulton County District Attorneys Office*)

June 5, 1996

To whom it may concern:

I have not had a chance to update my will prior to Ms. Baugh asking me to put something in writing regarding the ownership of the Mercedes C220.

The Mercedes C220 Serial #WDBHA22E9TF331602 purchased on 5/31/96 belongs to Ms. Baugh. I am financing it for her because she did not have good credit to finance it on her own. She gave me $4,000 as the initial down payment and I put the rest and make the monthly payments. As soon as Ms. Baugh is able to make the monthly payments hopefully by April 1997 she will takeover making the monthly payments, until then I will continue to make the payments for her.

In the event of my death the car should be released to Ms. Baugh and Nationsbank should be contacted to release the title to Ms. Baugh. This vehicle should not be considered a part of my personal asset although I am financing it, as it belongs to Ms. Baugh. I love her and I am helping her.

Typed by: Dionne Baugh

Signed by: Lance H. Herndon

21-0019-24-97

Investigators noted that on the same day that Lance Herndon's body was discovered, his credit card had also been used to purchase a mahogany cabinet from a luxury furniture gallery in North Carolina. Records of the telephone transaction indicated that Dionne Baugh fraudulently posed as Dionne "Herndon" during the purchase. (*Courtesy of Fulton County District Attorneys Office*)

Prison mug shot of Dionne.
(*Courtesy of the Georgia Department of Corrections*)

PHYSICAL DESCRIPTION			
YOB: 1968	RACE: BLACK		GENDER: FEMALE
HEIGHT: 5' 04"	WEIGHT: 131	EYE COLOR: BROWN	HAIR COLOR: BROWN

INCARCERATION DETAILS	
MAJOR OFFENSE: VOLUNTARY MANSLAUGHTER	
MOST RECENT INSTITUTION: PULASKI STATE PRISON (W)	
MAX POSSIBLE RELEASE DATE:	07/28/2011
TENTATIVE PAROLE MONTH:	07/2010
ACTUAL RELEASE DATE:	CURRENTLY SERVING
CURRENT STATUS:	ACTIVE

KNOWN ALIASES
A.K.A. BAUGH, DIONNE
A.K.A. NELSON, DIONNE ANDREA

STATE OF GEORGIA - CURRENT SENTENCES	
CASE NO:	469990
OFFENSE:	VOLUNTARY MANSLAUGHTER
CONVICTION COUNTY:	FULTON COUNTY
CRIME COMMITMENT DATE:	08/08/1996
SENTENCE LENGTH:	10 YEARS, 0 MONTHS, 0 DAYS

STATE OF GEORGIA - PRIOR SENTENCES	
STATE OF GEORGIA - INCARCERATION HISTORY	
INCARCERATION BEGIN	INCARCERATION END
05/07/2001	ACTIVE

With the jury now peering skeptically at him, Clint offered an example. "Let's say you leave here tonight, and get in your car. You're driving up 85 and you see the gas light come on. Oh, Lord, you think, I'm on empty. I've got to stop and get some gas. So you pull off the highway to a gas station and drive up to the pump. You pull out your credit card, pay for the gas, pull the nozzle out, open up your gas cap, put the nozzle in, and you hear the machine start to whir. You feel the hose jerk. And you see the numbers start to turn on the gas tank. You can hear something gushing out of the hose. You take the hose out, put it back on the machine, and put your gas cap back on. You get in your car, start it up, and drive off. You did not see the gas go into your car, and you didn't get up underneath the car to make sure the gas was going in there, did you? No, because just as with the evidence in this case, based on your personal experiences, some good common sense, and the facts from which you can infer other facts—such as I've been to this gas station five hundred times before and, every time, I get gas—even though you don't see it, you can rely on those facts and drive off feeling very comfortable that your tank is full."

The jury could see in Rucker's eyes that it all made sense to him. He knew what happened to Lance Herndon, had connected all the dots that explained how Lance died that night. Nobody imagined it more clearly than him, but the jury, too, was starting to absorb his vision.

Lance took Dionne's waist, easing her toward him. This time she did not resist, but rather leaned over and slid her head beneath the sheets to offer him the oral pleasure to which he had become so accustomed. She stayed there for several minutes, not out of desire but something more sustaining. It was fear. Not the fear of losing the man. She had a man. But the fear of losing the material things, the privilege, he bought her. She heard him moaning from what seemed like a great distance, and when she heard him cry out, she could not stand to face him but instead rested there on his moist thigh until she heard the steady, breathy rhythm of him sleeping.

As he slept, Dionne slid out of bed, stepped quietly out of the bedroom, and padded quickly down the stairs to the office, her nude shadow moving through the darkness of his home. Pausing on the landing of the second level, she noticed a nightlight glowing in one of the bedrooms, and for the first time, it dawned on her that Lance's grandmother was in that room asleep, and so her steps became more gingerly as she descended the stairs into the office. She could not help herself: she did not trust that Lance was planning to show up in court tomorrow. She needed to verify the appointment for herself on his calendar. She had been in the Access suite often enough to be familiar with its setup, and she stepped directly into Lance's private office, sat down at his computer, and typed a few keystrokes. As the itinerary for August 8, 1996, glowed on the screen, her limbs tightened.

There was nothing. Nothing! Dionne rose from the desk and walked toward the staircase.

Clint stepped over and flipped a few pages in his notebook, jabbing his ballpoint emphatically at one of the pages. "There were footprints going toward the door, and footprints going away from the door," he said. "About a size eight and half. I submit to you that those are the footprints of the killer when she went over there to pick up this wrench from off the floor that was in his bedroom by the balcony." If Clint knew this statement to be an exaggeration, that the footprints were large enough for investigators to assume they were male in origin, he showed no such sign. "The evidence in the case," Clint went on, "has shown that the killer was on the bed. The killer was up close and personal when taking Mr. Herndon's life. The killer struck him first from the back."

*D*ionne stood over Lance as he slept. In her right hand was a long, silver wrench. The erotic video had played through and the screen had gone dark and the room was quiet. She stared at him for a moment, peering with contempt at the man who mistook her for his fool. Sensing her hovering, Lance's eyes opened groggily, and his head rose off the pillow. It was too late. Dionne, as though splitting wood with an ax, brought the wrench crashing down on Lance's head. He fell back, and she leapt on him, her legs straddling his chest. Again, she brought the wrench down hard on his face, and this time blood gushed up on her. She could not stop herself, though. She swung the wrench down again, harder this time, and then again so that soon the face beneath her was no longer one that she recognized but a mash of flesh and bone and blood.

*C*lint was standing before the jury holding in his hands the exhibit—the large crescent wrench—striking his palm with it. His mock murder weapon, lampooned moments ago, had now taken on a terrible realness. "He was struck again and again and again and again and again, as many as fourteen times, until she beat the life out of him," he said. "We know that she touched his bloody body with her hands when she got up. And we know she laid the weapon down on the sheet. If you have any doubt about that . . ." Rucker stepped over to the projector and brought the bloody crime-scene photo onto the screen. "Look at that. Look at that," he said. "The blood stain on this sheet fits perfectly and is consistent with the carpet impression near that balcony door."

Clint strode back over to the jury and pointed over at Dionne. "And what you have to figure is that after she beat him, beat the life out of him, she is covered with the fine mist of his blood. Probably some brain tissue as well, which is what the medical examiner said. And what she does is grab the pillow from the top of the bed, and brings it to the foot of the bed. She takes the pillowcase off, and she uses it to wipe off with. We know she doesn't have on any clothes because she left the pubic hair on this man's chest, on his bloody chest. The hair can't just mysteriously jump out of your underwear, out of your pants, and then mysteriously land on his body. Just use your common sense. Then she puts the pillowcase in the commode."

*H*er *nude body spattered with blood, Dionne leaned over and turned on the bathtub faucet. Waiting for the tub to fill up with warm water, she walked back out into the bedroom and stepped over to Lance's bludgeoned body. She reached over and tilted Lance's head to the side to unclasp his gold necklace. Then she pulled the sheet up over his body, before heading back to the bathroom and soaking her own clean of Lance's blood.*

*S*he is evil," Clint thundered, shaking his fist at the jury. "She takes time to rifle through his dresser to get a credit card. She unplugs the phone from the wall. And then she takes the time to unplug all three alarm clocks. Who would do that but a killer who is familiar with the victim? And then she takes the additional step of wiping everything down with the pants he had on that day. She wraps the wrench up in them too. That's why we can't find them. Lance lived by his pager. We found the pager in the foyer on the floor. Because that's where it fell off his belt when she was going out the door. That's also why you have change scattered right there on the floor. That all came out of his pants. And before she leaves the house, she thinks, Let me go downstairs and get this computer, the one I borrowed a few times to do some schoolwork. Lance won't need it anymore. Nobody will ever know."

Clint moved closer to the jury, taking the time to look at them each individually.

"But she was wrong," he said, his voice calm now.

Clint picked up the glass jar and held it up to the jury. The water sparkled pure under the bright light of the courtroom. "We know she killed Lance Herndon," he said. "The facts are clear, just like the water in this jar. Convict this defendant of each and every count in the state's bill of indictment.

"Do not let her escape. Thank you."

chapter eighteen

THE DUES THING

Juror Ben Wilson is a self-proclaimed country boy, a tobacco-chewing southerner who grew up hunting and fishing in his native Johnson City, Tennessee, a mountain community in the state's northeast corner, near the North Carolina border. He was just a youngster when he brought home his first deer, which he "popped right on the side with a bow and arrow fifteen minutes after the sun came up." Four years at the University of Georgia, where he studied computers while on a tennis scholarship, and then three more years among the white-collars at his job as a software salesman had not changed his rural sensibility, let alone prepared him to empathize with the tribulations of a character like Lance Herndon. "I just couldn't relate to the guy at all," Wilson said. "He had everything a man would ever want, but he was a real idiot. He blew all his money trying to win people over." Wilson chuckled, then added sarcastically, "And when it came to women, hey, the man was pretty much a pimp."

But as Wilson took his seat among the other eleven jurors for deliberation that April morning, he tried to push whatever negative personal feelings he harbored about Herndon's lifestyle out of his mind and simply deal with the facts put before him. He even tried to forget—although he knew this wasn't possible—how spellbound he and the other jurors had been during Clint's theatrical closing argument, over the prosecutor's stirring oratory, smart analysis, and, of course, that nice touch with the water and sand. Wilson tried not to let any of these things distract him from the only question of real consequence. And on this matter, Wilson believed Dionne was guilty.

While Wilson wasn't the foreman, he was the most outspoken of the jury, and it didn't take him long at all to bring fellow jurors to see his point of view: of the suspects, Baugh was the only one with the motive and opportunity to kill Lance Herndon. It took the jury only a couple of hours before they returned with a verdict; guilty of one count of felony murder, one count of aggravated assault, two counts of theft by taking, and one count of financial fraud.

The verdict sent tremors throughout the courtroom; joyful cries erupted from the Herndon family as Jackie Herndon and Jeannine leapt out of their seats, embracing, relieved and teary-eyed. There were muted sobs from Dionne's family. Both Gerry Quinn and Michael Katz rested a hand on Dionne's shoulder. Her expression was difficult to read; she stared straight ahead, eyes moist, unblinking. She looked over at her family. Then she wept softly.

———

On the morning Dionne was to be sentenced, Gerry Quinn asked for permission to approach the bench. Stepping up to face Judge Baxter, Quinn made a motion for a mistrial. His reason: he had learned that Clint Rucker had not paid his annual dues for that year to the State Bar of Georgia, a lapse that, in effect, made him ineligible to practice law in the state and thereby disqualified him from prosecuting Dionne Baugh.

Clint was mortified. He had expected some kind of legal challenge, as several moments during the trial seemed to invite as much. There were a couple of incidents of direct- and cross-examinations in which his witnesses had breached the court's strict orders to avoid offering hearsay evidence regarding Lance Herndon's statements or state of mind days before his murder. And late in the trial there had been a few times, too, when Clint may have gone too far in his examination of Detective Anastasio, guiding him to bolster the credibility of other witnesses. But grief over paying his bar dues; this he had not expected.

The disclosure shrouded Clint in a depressing irony. Over the next few hours, Clint Rucker, the star black prosecutor, found himself up on the witness stand defending himself against the most rudimentary, if not embarrassing, charges one can hurl at an attorney. Jurors looked deflated: here was their hero, who had, in a sense, triumphantly reached the mountaintop to light the torch, and now, with the world gazing up at him, he was fumbling around in his pocket for a match. His sin, of course, was exacerbated inside the unspoken subtext of race by the stereotype that blacks all too often place style above substance. The transgression had eerily placed him in the mold of Lance. Worse still, no matter how minor his infraction or even its perception, Clint's had occurred in the most hallowed and transparent of public arenas. While it was ostensibly framed as a legal argument over the necessity of paying one's bar dues, the issue served to vindicate Clint's colleagues for doubting his real value in the profession.

Quinn pulled few punches in grilling Clint for what he called an egregious disregard for perhaps the most sacred requirement in practicing law, which was maintaining a record of good standing with the state bar. "Mr. Rucker, you will admit, won't you, that at the time we started this trial, you were not in good standing with the state bar?"

"Yes. That appears to be the case."

"And you had not paid your dues. That's the reason?"

"Yes. That also appears to be the case."

Quinn went on to ask, wryly, "Do you agree with the proposition that you should be required to play by the same rules that I play by?"

"Yes."

"One of the things you swore to do was to uphold the law, correct?"

"Yes."

"And it is not upholding the law to come up here and try a case when you are not authorized to do it, is it?"

Judge Baxter joined in the drubbing. "Mr. Rucker," he fumed, "do you understand that every lawyer in the state pays their dues every year? I have done it for twenty-eight years. I mean, you just *pay* your dues. There is nothing real hard about that. And if you don't, then you are not supposed to practice law. Do you understand that? What do you not understand about that?"

"I understand that, your honor," Rucker replied sheepishly.

"So I'm just wondering why we are in this position. I mean, do you have any excuse or explanation for why we are sitting here doing this?"

"I am personally embarrassed, your honor, and—"

"Well, I'm sorry," Baxter snapped.

"No. I take full responsibility. It was an oversight on my part, and it is inexcusable, and it will never happen again."

"I hope not."

In further examination, Quinn raked Rucker over so hard that Baxter eventually cut him off, seemingly out of sheer pity. "Mr. Quinn, we have beat Mr. Rucker enough, and I would say he doesn't deserve it. We have beat him enough!"

It would suffice to say that Clint got an embarrassing dressing-down that morning. He was contrite enough, as he tried to explain away the matter as an innocent bookkeeping oversight, insisting that, contrary to testimony by officials of the State Bar of Georgia, he couldn't recall receiving several warnings via phone messages and mail of suspension for unpaid dues.

Judge Baxter was incredulous at such excuses. "Mr. Rucker, you tried this case," he said. "You remember minute details. You presented this case in a masterful way, and you are sitting here telling the court you don't remember receiving those calls when you remember evidence, names, and presented this case that lasted ten days? Are you telling me that you don't remember any of this, and you expect me to believe that? Are you telling me that?"

"Yes, sir, your honor," Rucker said.

The episode left bitter feelings for nearly all involved. Nearly a year later, Gerry Quinn was still grumbling over it. "I see the raw talent that Clint has, and the power he's got as a lawyer," he says one afternoon at his office in Decatur. "But it's like, winning is everything to him. That's how I was when I was younger, and Clint is not quite out of that stage. He doesn't think about the other things that in the long run are more important. C'mon, you're the main prosecutor who handles the murder cases in this county, all the big notoriety cases, and you sit there and say that you *forgot* to pay your dues. It was no different than you or any layperson coming in off the street and trying a case. Basically, what he was saying is, I don't have to pay my dues. I don't need a license. It showed arrogance and indifference—that the same rules that apply to the rest of us don't apply to Clint. . . . I felt horrible for the Herndon family. You could just see the pain in their faces. Their guy had just brought them victory and now was also about to take it away from them."

Paul Howard could only shake his head in disgust when asked about the matter. "The guy is just so full of contradictions," he said of his protégé. "It's like, 'Man, you've finally gotten yourself to a point that people honestly recognize you for what you are, which is one of the most skilled trial attorneys in this state and probably in this country, and jackass, you forget to pay your damn dues?' But that's Clint. That's how he is. That's his personality. He drives me absolutely crazy because he is always late with something. He's the kind of person you have to have an intern working with him twenty-four hours a day to make sure he's on task. He's just disorganized. I guess you might say he's the opposite of Lance Herndon.

"He's almost like a musician, an entertainer. They are on a different frequency. I'm sure people have been flabbergasted with Miles Davis, but when they are so talented, what can you do? I'll chew him out, and he'll tell me he won't do it again, and then he does it all over again. He can't help it. He just won't do anything on time. He's terrific in many ways, but he's driving me crazy, and I keep telling him, you've got one more damn time, just one more. When the bar thing happened, I called him into my office. I demoted him and cut his pay."

Over breakfast one morning, Clint had less insight than Howard about his dues fiasco. He didn't have a good story. The right words did not come pouring out of him. "I cannot ever remember feeling as bad as I did after that," he said softly. "Ever in my life. I really felt bad for the Herndon family, that they had to deal with what was clearly my own negligence. That was really hard for me. You have to understand that from the first moment I ever met them, I don't think they ever really believed in me. They didn't believe that the evidence was good enough, and I don't think they thought I was an experienced enough lawyer to get a conviction. But let me tell you something, from the time I got the case in late 1996, I had grown into a very different lawyer than the one that ultimately tried the case in 2001. I had learned how to really deliver in court, and I think the family was surprised by that. They were on a high and thought I did a really good job, and then . . ." Clint's voice faded to silence.

"I felt really bad for my team, Anna and Phyllis, because nobody ever really got a chance to stand up and tell us what a good job we did. And I felt bad for Mr. Howard, because what I've always learned from him is that *we* have to be better, and I think his biggest disappointment with me is that he understands that *we* have to be above and beyond. The standard is higher for us. When you don't recognize that and adjust accordingly, it's kind of like you give *them* the opportunity to do what they will. I think that's where Mr. Howard was coming from. He was like, 'C'mon man, they caught you. It's like we always get busted on the same shit, even though we *know* that they are looking.' And when you put that in the context of the office, which is a very competitive, 'I can't fail' environment, and then I have this huge failure, it was bad. I mean, I'm not just Joe Q. Prosecutor over there. Whether it's true or not, they see me as Paul Howard's son, the Chosen One."

Cocounsel Anna Green defended Clint in court that day. "If Mr. Quinn wants to talk about playing by the same rules, let's play by the same rules," she argued to Judge Baxter. "If Mr. Quinn had not paid his bar dues, that would not render him ineffective, as far as in-validating any action he took on the part of the defendant. Same thing goes for Mr. Rucker. He is a de facto public official whether he paid his bar dues or didn't pay his bar dues.

"... He handled this trial well.... We are talking about a minor administrative infraction.... Mr. Rucker handled the majority of the case in front of this jury, but he was one of three duly autho-rized assistant district attorneys sitting at the prosecution table. The jurisdiction to try this defendant rests with the district attorney's office, not Mr. Rucker, not myself, not any one individual. It is the office that has jurisdiction, who prosecuted Ms. Baugh, and who se-cured a conviction for the murder of Lance Herndon and all the charges in the indictment."

Clearly exasperated by the turn of events, Judge Baxter looked down from the bench at Gerry Quinn. Having listened to Anna Green's argument and after considering various questions around legal precedent and double jeopardy, he decided to overrule the de-fense's motion for a mistrial. "I think the Supreme Court of Geor-gia will definitely be looking at this," the judge told Gerry Quinn almost apologetically. "They are the ultimate arbitrator of these rules, and the state has given you a giant appealable issue. There are a lot of wise people up there. A lot wiser than I am. And they will tell you what all this means. But I'm going to allow the verdict to stand, and we are ready for sentencing in this case."

It was shortly thereafter that Jeannine Herndon, offering a cus-tomary victim-impact statement, stood, her voice quivering. "Your honor, for the court, I speak for myself, representing my son, John Harrison Herndon, and for Jackie Herndon. The impact that this had made on this family, for a mother who found her son . . ." She paused. "Her comment to me and to her friends and family is that, basically, her life is finished now because this is the worst of the worst that could happen. Nothing could be worse than finding your child like that. It's felt all the time. She says when she wakes in the morning, his face is the first thing that she sees, and it is the first thing she sees when she goes to bed."

Jeannine Herndon's voice cracked as she continued. "For my son . . . Well, my son has lost his father," she said. "He misses him. He doesn't understand why this happened. And for a long time, he would ask me why God would take his father.

"How does this impact us? It will impact us for the rest of our lives."

When Jeannine Herndon had finished, the judge handed down Dionne's sentence, imposing a term of life imprisonment for the murder of Lance Harrison Herndon. He also ordered sentences for the lesser charges of theft and credit card fraud, to run concurrently.

"Let that be the conviction," the judge said.

With those words, the system had mechanically performed its intended function of reducing complex human foible into a simple measured penalty. For all involved, the verdict was sadly anticlimactic in its matter-of-factness. The courtroom was quiet. The defendant stared straight ahead. Then the court's deputy sheriff stepped over to Dionne Baugh. "This way, ma'am."

Judge Baxter rubbed his eyes. "All right," he said. "Court is in recess."

Clint Rucker, celebrated practitioner of jurisprudence though he may be, is certainly not much of a drinker. Standing at the bar, a long line of thirsty customers waiting impatiently behind him, Clint scowls at the row of spirits lined up in front of him, as though picking medicine for a dying village. Finally, exhausted by his own indecision, he blurts out a beverage.

"Gimme a rum and Coke."

The bartender rolls his eyes. "Whatever, man. Eight bucks."

Clint cuts into the crowd, his eyes drawn to a leggy woman striding by in a fire-engine-red suede miniskirt and high matching boots. Sweetly fragranced, she preens past, curvaceous and sliding across dim light. Clint blinks hard. "This is no way for a man to live," he says, smiling.

For the past three days, under the banner of the annual NBA All-Star Weekend, downtown Atlanta has morphed into something resembling a rap music video. Clogging the streets, hotels, and bars are young black men and women, their devotion to the gods of high-flying dunks and high-priced sneakers giving rise to a Mardi Gras–like celebration along Peachtree and the surrounding blocks. Blaring from car stereos in the chilly February air is the boom of heavy bass drums and sermonizing gangstas, their disciples leaning behind the steering wheels of chromed-out Hummers and Escalades, of low-riding Chevys that bounce and shimmy at stoplights.

Inside the Georgia World Congress Center is the weekend's most exclusive bash, the NBA Players Association party, where a diamond-studded, fur-coated, leather-clad, alligator-shoed mosaic of ghetto fabulousness is on display. Drawn to the extravaganza is an eclectic mix of thrill seekers. Striding in, a few feet over, is President Bill Clinton himself, dressed in a dark suit sans necktie, Secret Service in tow. There, just yards away from the former leader of the free world, is the former leader of the Lakers' fast break, point guard Norm Nixon, and his wife, actress and dance choreographer Debbie Allen. At the entrance, pushing his way to the front of the snaking line is baseball legend Dave Winfield, ostensibly displeased that his batting prowess has not gained him prompt entry into the party.

Indeed, as Lance once fretted, the hip-hop era has ceremoniously arrived in this city without him. Onstage, a rather aged Gap Band performs live music, the group's real drums and trumpets and electric guitars tacked on to this ticket as a counterbalance to a night of otherwise synthetic bass lines, four-letter soliloquies, and borrowed melodies. As the once-famous seventies band belts out "You Dropped a Bomb on Me," the throngs of baggy-suited homeboys and form-fitted homegirls exchange expressions of horror and bemusement, like tourists thrust into black music's version of *Jurassic Park*.

The city's star culture, once owned by Toni Braxton and Regina Belle and TLC, has changed hands to the likes of Usher, Outkast, and Ludacris and producers such as Jermaine Dupri and Dallas Austin. Big money is exchanging hands, too. SunTrust Bank, among the largest financial institutions in the Southeast, has even formed a private banking group in Atlanta, now dubbed the hip-hop mecca. For street cred, the bank boasts a radically new approach to business. "We don't want this to feel like a bank to them," one SunTrust executive told a local reporter. "We want them to talk to us, whether it's about their next business venture or their baby's-momma drama." Instead of the traditional decor, the division has gold and platinum music awards on the walls, and music videos playing on the television. The bank's clients, discovered and cultivated by scouting the local nightclubs, are encouraged to flout traditional business etiquette and drop by at will during the workday or even call their bankers at home late into the night if necessary.

"You know, Lance would have definitely been out tonight," Clint muses to me. "He would have bought a boatload of tickets to the game, given them out to all his friends, and rented some big hotel suite and hosted an after-party. As far as I know, the man wasn't even a basketball fan, but he definitely would have figured out a way to be on the scene tonight."

————

Hours after the NBA shindig, Clint and I find ourselves at another hot party, this one in a warehouse in Buckhead where Reebok is celebrating the launch of rapper Jay-Z's new sneaker. Buckhead is an old North Atlanta neighborhood of rolling, tree-canopied streets—the "Beverly Hills of the South," it has been called. There was a time when Buckhead's bars were populated by college frat boys, but now the area—to the chagrin of the community's well-heeled residents—is known as a stomping ground for hip-hoppers.

Late-night skirmishes have become somewhat common in Buckhead. The most infamous incident, of course, was a shooting that involved Baltimore Ravens defensive star Ray Lewis and left two men dead. The Ray Lewis melee, which occurred after a Super Bowl, is still a sore topic for Clint, who initially led the prosecution of the NFL star but was pushed aside mid-trial by DA Paul Howard, who decided to try the case himself. His courtroom skills rusty, Paul Howard showboated his way into embarrassment for the DA's office as Lewis and his friends were cleared of the most serious charges.

Inside, the Buckhead warehouse has vaulted ceilings, cinder-block walls, and almost no ventilation. And the place is packed. Late into the night, surrounded by bodyguards, Jay-Z, dressed in a blue jogging suit and baseball cap, eases his way in with his stiletto-heeled singer Beyoncé beside him. The couple disappears into a roped-off VIP area. As Clint pushes his way through the standing-room-only crowd, the music is deafening.

Dressed in blazer and slacks, Clint and I look out of place. On the dance floor are girls with flat midriffs and lowrider jeans gyrating suggestively to rap music, guys in baseball caps and Timberland boots dipping and prowling coolly around them. Native rapper Ludacris's drawling anthem to the local nightlife has the club bouncing.

> *Welcome to Atlanta, where the players play*
> *And we ride on dem thangs like ev-ery day*
> *Big beats, hit streets, see gangsters roamin*
> *And the parties don't stop till eight in the mo 'nin*

We hang out for a while, but soon have had enough. Outside, the air is brisk, the sky moonlit. Clint scouts for a taxi, sees none, and starts walking, the skyline glowing ahead. A few quiet blocks later, he breaks his stride and grins. He returns to his favorite subject. "People have asked me how I was able to see my way through the Dionne thing," he says. "How I knew that a woman could actually do something like that."

Clint starts walking again. "Back when I was in college at Emory, I was dating this fine honey. I swear, all the fellas were jealous because she was just a perfect ten. Super smart in the classroom, a star on the track team, and had a body that would straight up knock you out. I mean, knock you *out*, bro. My frat brothers were just waiting for me to mess that up, so they could have a chance.

"The only thing was her temper, though. I mean, she would just snap on you, dawg, like, over nothing. Like we'd be at a party, and she'd just get tired and be ready to leave and come over and like tell me it was time to leave now. My boys would look at me, like damn, dawg, your girl is tripping. But she was so fine, I just kinda played it off, you know. It wasn't like she was like that all the time. But now and then, that temper would snap without warning. She'd get pissed about something and lose it completely, swinging and kicking at me.

"Anyway, one night we were at my mom's, and I was sitting

there in the kitchen filling out law school applications, not giving my girl enough attention, I guess. She got pissed at me and—"

Clint stops in his tracks and swings his arm in a fast slapping motion. "Bam!"

He tosses his head back, as though in pain. "I didn't know what hit me. I swear, I wanted to kill that girl. But I just jumped up and held her back, and she was wailing at me like a crazy woman. Things got so loud that my mother got up from bed, ran downstairs, and pulled us off each other. Then my mother got dressed and drove her home. When she got back, my mom was was fuming. She was like, 'Clint, you've gotta let that girl go. She's outta her mind and she's gonna drive you crazy too.' Then she did what she always did whenever she thought I was being dumb. She tapped her knuckles on my forehead, 'When are you gonna start using that gray matter inside your head? God gave it to you for a reason, you know?'

"Anyway, I broke it off and went on to law school. But I saw her when I graduated. She had married this police officer, a real nice brother. I'd always see him over at the courthouse. Me and him actually got to be kind of cool. He had a little security firm on the side. He was just a really, really nice guy. Anyway, one day I was watching the news, I see on there that he has gone and pulled out a revolver, killed her and then himself. They hadn't been married but a year. There wasn't a question in my mind that she drove him to it. She snapped on that man one too many times, and he killed her."

Clint raises his hand, and a taxi cruises up to the curbside. "I just figure Lance never got that chance, you know," he says, stepping into the taxi. "Dionne killed him instead."

epilogue

Dionne Baugh's hair is parted in the center and pulled back severely in a bun. Her eyes are sunken and placid, observing me with suspicion. Her lips are plump, bow-shaped, her nose closer to broad than keen. It is only the combination of the full lips and wide nose that reveals her as black, because her skin is pale, almost ivory in hue. She is quite thin; all shoulders, knees, and elbows. On her feet are white sweat socks and thong sandals.

The longer I look at her, the more I realize that it is not her unremarkable appearance that is a letdown, but her deeply affected manner. With her legs crossed and hands folded across her lap, you'd swear this prim soul wasn't in prison gear doing hard time but arriving in Chanel for a tea party. Even as she begins to describe her life over the past two years, it is in a voice dripping with condescension, the measured words of a misunderstood queen among a prison population of paupers. The other women here are rough and unrefined, she shares at one point, and constantly picking fights with her. Jealous, she figures.

When I inquire about why, I get the familiar skin-color diatribe. In her faint Jamaican accent, she explains that her fair skin has been a burden since she moved to the States. "Atlanta is mostly just black and white," she says. "If you fall somewhere in between, then you find yourself outcast. I am a black woman, so I had the whites hating me because I'm not really white, and the blacks hating me too because I'm not black. Atlanta is divided between light-skinned blacks and dark-skinned blacks, which is the craziest thing I've ever seen in my life. Back in Jamaica, there was more of a class differentiation; it's about your last name and whether your family is affluent or not. You could be black as tar and be considered to be high-class as long as you have the right last name. Here, people are just confused. I would always get the question, 'Are you black or white?' But I didn't care. I know who I am."

I ask how she is holding up in prison—wrongly accused, as she claims to be. A flicker ignites somber eyes. "I actually can see the light at the end of the tunnel," she says somewhat merrily. "I'm doing much better than I was. It was hard at first, but once I got to the prison I started studying the Bible with the other Jehovah's Witnesses, and I remember reading, I think it's Ecclesiastes 9:11, where I believe it says that 'time and unforeseen circumstances will befall us all.' So once you start looking at it from that perspective, I'm not the first person that this happened to and I won't be the last. I just read about a man who was wrongly accused of killing this young lady, and he went into a second trial, and once again he was convicted, and like ten years later they actually found the person who really did it."

When I inquire about her daughter Amanda and how she is

coping with not being part of the girl's daily life, Dionne Baugh reacts as if a blade has cut into her. Her face contorts, her head drops. She breaks down sobbing. "Please," she says, burying her face in her hands. "Don't ask me about my daughter." She cries for quite some time. Charles Mittelstadt, a criminal investigator hired to collect evidence to strengthen her case, shoots me a look of disapproval. I sit quietly and let the moment pass. Trying to switch to a more cheerful subject, I ask what she expects her life to be like on the outside if she is granted her freedom, whether she will leave Atlanta.

"I'm undecided about that," she says. "Initially, I wanted to leave—to just get out. But there's another side of me that's like, I haven't done anything. Why move? Why run away? I just want to put this behind me."

She thinks awhile and goes on. "But I'm a private person, and I've been disgraced enough," she says. "Whatever people think they know about me, they're wrong. They really don't know me. If that is the perception that they want to have, then let them have that."

She laughs. It is a high-spirited laugh, youthful like a teenager's. "But I'm feeling good," she says. "I have a league of extraordinary gentlemen behind me now, so I know things are going to work out."

Charles Mittelstadt asks me to wait a few minutes in the corridor so he can confer privately with Dionne about her upcoming trial. The door slams shut, and I am left there alone to reflect on Dionne Baugh, who seems to me now to be little more than a dissembler, not unlike Lance himself. I am left alone to reflect on small matters, like the dank smell of prison, and larger ones, such as the foibles of men like Lance Herndon, the black and fabulous, or, as W. E. B. DuBois more regally dubbed them, the Talented Tenth. Only now does it occur to me that while DuBois was busy snubbing the blue-collar rhetoric of men like Booker T. Washington, sermonizing about how only the most ambitious cadre of blacks could spirit the race toward real freedom, he failed to consider the competing allure of the ménage à trois, the Nordstrom sale, and gold diggers like Dionne. He failed to predict how in the twentieth century a man like Lance Herndon, an enthusiast of these empty pursuits, might come to embody the crisis of wasted intellectual and moral capital in our race.

Of course, DuBois had been dead on about one thing. "Atlanta must not lead the South to dream of material prosperity as the touchstone of all success," he wrote in his 1903 race classic *The Souls of Black Folk;* ". . . already the fatal might of this idea is beginning to spread; it is replacing the finer type of Southerner with vulgar money-getters; it is burying the sweeter beauties of Southern life beneath pretense and ostentation."

I can't help but marvel at how a warning intended for whites at the turn of the century would be so prophetic for blacks by the end of it.

afterword

In July 2003, the Georgia Supreme Court overturned Dionne Baugh's conviction due to improper "hearsay" testimony provided by Detective Anastasio. Baugh's November 2003 retrial ended in a deadlocked jury, and a mistrial was declared. As a third trial was set to begin in September 2004, Baugh pleaded guilty to the lesser charge of voluntary manslaughter. She was sentenced to ten years in state prison.

acknowledgments

Like the city of Atlanta, this book has experienced several essential incarnations. At each stage, its author has benefited from the talent, devotion, and wisdom of many. I am especially grateful to William Anastasio, the APEX Museum, William Grady Ashworth, Jimmie Bailey, Stacey Barney, Jerry Baxter, Tina Beyene, Keith Clinkscales, Julie Dearborn, Cheryl Carol, Katherine Donaldson, Eugene Duffy, Jeff Garigliano, Annette Gendler, Nadira A. Hira, Paul Howard, John Huey, Daphne Bryson Jackson, Gary Jenkins, Michael Katz, Jim Kelly, Anne Kornblatt, Fred Leebron, Andrew Levy, Suzannah Lessard, Rebecca McClanahan, Charles Mittelstadt, J.R. Moehringer, Christina Morgan, Andrew Park, Evelyn Parker, Robert Polito, Kent Priestley, Krisseda Pryor, Robert Pryor, Mike Ross, Bunnie Jackson-Ransom, Clint Rucker, Sheila Saints, The Schaumburg Library, Ronald Stodghill, Sr., Don Samuel, Dena Smith, Edith Stanley, Louise Springer, Peter Stitt, Jason Tanz, Angela Thornton, Queens University of Charlotte, Gerry Quinn, Kimberly Stodghill Walker, A. Scott Walton,

Jonathan Webb, Morgan Welebir, Ann Wicker, and Carolyn Zolas.

Thank you also to my agents, Jane Dystel and Miriam Goderich, and to my publicist, Robin Davis. And to my brilliant editor, Dawn Davis, who, along with Tracy Sherrod, understood my vision and guided the work to its completion. I am, of course, forever indebted to my loving wife, Robyn, a constant source of creative energy, support, and inspiration.

And to God from whom all blessings flow.

about the author

Ron Stodghill is a staff writer with the *New York Times*. He was educated at the University of Missouri and Harvard University, where he was a Nieman Fellow. His work has appeared in *Time, BusinessWeek, Reader's Digest, Essence,* and several newspapers. A former editor in chief of *Savoy* magazine, Stodghill lives in Charlotte, North Carolina, with his wife and three sons.